DAVID SHEPHERD
My Painting Life

DAVID SHEPHERD
My Painting Life

AUTHORS NOTE

When the idea of a collection of my paintings was first conceived, I thought that it would be a simple matter of just selecting some seventy pictures out of more than three thousand that I have painted so far. As time went by, the project grew alarmingly in scale. Not only did I realise very quickly how difficult it would be to choose which ones would make up a representative selection, but as I reflected on each painting, I recalled so many memories and anecdotes that I found myself tempted to write a book on each.

No discourtesy is intended if the ownership of some paintings is not acknowledged. It is simply that over the years many of my pictures have changed hands and I no longer know where they are. I feel that it is most appropriate, therefore, to thank everyone and I hope that you are not too surprised if you discover your painting reproduced in this book.

Book designed by Michael Head
Typeset by XL Publishing Services. Nairn
Printed In Singapore by Saik Wah Press Pte Ltd
Jointly Published by RD & AS Shepherd Partnership, Brooklands Farm
Hammerwood, East Grinstead, West Sussex. United Kingdom RH19 3QA
and Zodiac Publishing. P.O.Box 35121, Dubai, United Arab Emirates

CONTENTS

From HRH The Prince Philip
Duke of Edinburgh KG, KT

BUCKINGHAM PALACE.

Lucky are those who can earn a living by doing what they enjoy; blessed are those who use their talents in a good cause.

Everyone committed to the conservation of nature and wildlife recognises the massive contribution that David Shepherd has made to this good cause.

From HRH Prince Bernhard
of the Netherlands

'I am very glad that this book has appeared. It will make many people familiar with my friend David Shepherd's beautiful paintings and will cause them to marvel at the wide variety of his subjects, which go from locomotives to wild animals. It was through the success of his wildlife paintings that David was able to buy his two locomotives, but, more importantly, he has also been able to raise funds for wildlife conservation to which he is truly devoted; this he has time and again proved in a most generous way. I, of course, wholeheartedly applaud this attitude!

'I sincerely hope that David will go on painting for years and years to come – not so much as a benefactor to wildlife, but as a source of pleasure to all his admirers, and for his own happiness and well-being.'

BERNHARD

From James Stewart
Hollywood

'David Shepherd's paintings of the environment and the wildlife of Africa have a certain dignity and class that are unmatched.'

JIMMY

From Frederick J.T. Chiluba
President of the Republic of Zambia

'As you have said yourself, your art owes much to all the inspiration given to you in the natural world, so that in return you feel obliged to give due measure of the rewards for your talent to wildlife conservation.

'With your paintings, you have given to Zambian wildlife as generously as you have received from the wildlife of our land.

'Truly, we are blessed who give as freely as we receive.'

FREDERICK J.T. CHILUBA

FOREWORD

I often WONDER whether David Shepherd ever stopped to think what would have happened to him if he had turned down the party invitation in 1950 when he met Robin Goodwin, the artist to whom, to quote his own words, 'I owe all my success'. What if Robin Goodwin hadn't turned up, or he and David had not been introduced? Perhaps David would by now have become Inspector Shepherd of London Transport Buses, the scourge of Route 88! Did fate do David Shepherd a good turn that night in 1950, or was it intended as a good turn for wildlife instead? Either way, it seems to have turned out very nicely for both parties on the whole!

As all benefactors know to their cost (quite literally in many cases), one generous gesture in aid of a good cause can be likened to throwing a little snowball on a mountainside only to bring an avalanche down on one's head! The good Shepherd has already raised, through his personal efforts and, in latter years, through the Conservation Foundation that bears his name, around £3,000,000 for conservation, plus hundreds of thousands of pounds for heritage and other causes which, he felt, merited his help. This generosity opened the floodgates to a tidal wave of appeals, and David has always found it very difficult to say 'No'.

By 1983, he realised that if he tried to grant all the requests for help, he would be working 24 hours a day non-stop for charity and not earning his keep. Good artists may not starve in garrets, but they need to pay their bills and look after their families just like everyone else. The situation was becoming desperate and it was beginning to affect David's routine commissions. As in days of old, David Shepherd was in need of some speedy assistance as he slowly disappeared under the avalanche of appeals.

The cause of David's problem was that he was trying to deal with all the appeals and requests personally, and suffering personal remorse and regret whenever he had to say no. The answer to this situation, as proposed by his friends, was quite simple. The David Shepherd Conservation Foundation, focusing on endangered mammals, was formed. David's life immediately became busier than ever and now he has told his own story in this book.

David and Avril Shepherd live in a beautiful sixteenth century farmhouse near the village of Hascombe in Surrey. With their family, they have been blessed with happiness and contentment in their home. In fact, the house itself is rich in character and has the feel of a dwelling that has been the centre of a great deal of joy and contentment throughout its 400 years of existence.

Do not imagine for one moment that the Shepherd household is as tranquil as the preceding paragraph may suggest. With his deep commitment to the two charities with which he is so closely connected, The David Shepherd Conservation Foundation, and The East Somerset Railway, the fact is that the house is 'mayhem', in David's own words, for most of the time, brought about by the very high level of entertaining and the number of people in the house which the charities generate' and with which Avril copes with astonishing ability.

All professors, scientists, biologists and artists are, by tradition, supposed to be absent-minded, emotional, petulant and, at times, hysterical! David is no exception to the rule, and he manages to combine all these traits with such skill and perfection that one could be forgiven for gaining the impression that they were the result of training and study!

This is where Avril Shepherd proves to be David's perfect partner, for while David crashes around the house like a rogue elephant with toothache looking for a letter or some other object which he is certain somebody has deliberately hidden - but which invariably turns up in his pocket - Avril goes quietly about the business of running the house, charming her guests and generally ignoring the crashes and thumps, the curses and ravings and slamming of doors.

David is quite magnificently flappable; Avril is supremely unflappable - and somehow this balance works wonderfully, as I have witnessed on so many occasions. The more nervous guests have been known to dive under the table or leap into cupboards as the roaring rogue elephant comes crashing into the room - only to settle in a chair, giggle like a naughty schoolboy and admit that whatever it was he was looking for was in his pocket all the time. As the trembling guests emerge from the cupboards and come up from under the table, they will almost certainly find Avril waiting to welcome them with a tray of (much needed) drinks at the ready and radiating that same brightness and tranquillity we experience when sunshine follows a thunderstorm!

The public image of David Shepherd is often that of a rather noisy and egotistical extrovert who must be absolute hell to live with. In fact, the real David is a surprisingly gentle and very genuine man who is quietly grateful for the wonderful gifts bestowed upon him, and grateful, too, to those who helped him to develop and bring out those creative talents which set him on the road to each success. It is a forty-year history of sheer hard work and dedication, with a liberal sprinkling of disappointments and set-backs, and a wonderful wife and family who share his successes and rally round whenever the rogue elephant has the toothache!

David Shepherd has so many acquaintances and friends all over the world that a wise man said of him, 'We may soon need his enemies to rally round and save him from his friends or he will become an endangered species'.

Fortunately for David, Avril, their four daughters and now their grandchildren and posterity, there are enough of David's real friends around to make sure that he does not become an endangered species. But he must still be hell to live with!

CYRIL LITTLEWOOD MBE
1995

GRANDPA'S WORKSHOP

When I met Bert Perriman, the friend who introduced us said, 'David, Bert will be sitting in his little shed at the bottom of his garden making a model steam engine, completely oblivious of everything else going on around him. I bet there is a clock on the shelf behind him.'

'Why?' I asked.

'Just wait and see,' was the reply.

Bert was sitting in his little shed, surrounded by the orderly chaos of the model maker – the tools, the lathe, and the inevitable Oxo tin, filled with bits and pieces and, sure enough,

on the shelf behind him was the clock. When Bert saw me looking at it, he said, 'My God, my wife asked me to mend that five years ago. I really must get on with it.' A lawnmower was sitting in the corner. He had obviously forgotten that as well.

MY EARLY YEARS

PAINTING PICTURES of elephants in Cornwall must sound a bit odd. However, this is what I used to do. Until a few years ago we had a lovely little 400-year-old thatched cottage and we used to try to get down there in the winter to escape from a busy life in Surrey. Even then I had a number of commissions so I would set my easel up in a little studio on the cliff top, next to the cottage, and paint wildlife. When I walked out of the studio carrying a wet elephant under my arm, the villagers must have thought I was completely dotty!

For some reason, those who know me seem to think that I am eccentric; I suppose I am in many ways. For example, my train set. Lots of small boys, and big boys too, have toy train sets, but mine is different. I have a habit of going for things in a rather big way and my locomotives weigh over 100 tons each. This might explain why I have been called 'The Man Who Loves Giants'; more about 'Black Prince' and 'The Green Knight' and the East Somerset Railway later. I am quite certain of one thing – I certainly didn't sit up in my pram the moment I was born and start drawing elephants.

London Life and World War II

I'm half Cornish and half Yorkshire – what a mixture. I was born more or less halfway between the two, in Hendon in North London and from a young age I was determined to make my mark. I gather that when I was about three years old, the local fire brigade had to come and rescue me with cutting equipment when I got my head stuck through the bars of our front gate. I must have been big-headed even in those early days.

Along with my sister and brother, our mum and dad used to cart me off to Birchington in Kent every summer, supposedly to build sand castles on the beach, like all good children, but Dad was super because he much preferred steam trains, thank goodness. So we used to go to the local level crossing to watch them go by. It was far more exciting than building sand castles.

I have never reasoned why, but it always seemed that horse-riding lessons were obligatory for children like us. We used to have our lessons in the Hertfordshire country-side which was beautifully unspoilt in those days. So many of the lovely places where we used to ride have now long since disappeared under ghastly concrete motor-ways. I suppose I enjoyed my riding lessons, but they had their awful moments of sheer terror. It seemed that I was always given the lazy or bloody-minded pony, it was always the one that lagged behind and finally came to a halt altogether. Then down would go its head and the wretched thing would start eating; at this point there was nothing I could do except scream for help as I began to slide down its neck. It would then wake up and shoot off at about 90 miles an hour to catch up with the rest of the class, with me hanging on for dear life. Indeed, the riding instructor seemed determined to kill me off at an early age. To me, the ponies were always far too big and the jumps even bigger.

I do have happy memories of those times as well. We used to go by train for lessons at a famous riding school near Maidenhead and although, like so many little boys, I always seemed to be sick on the journey, it had its compensations because the train was always drawn by a Great Western Railway steam engine.

Just before World War II we moved to Totteridge in North London and it was here that I took my first 'artistic' steps. While there had never been any artists in the family, and I had no artistic talent whatsoever, I entered a children's painting competition when I was eight years old. It was featured in a magazine called *The Nursery World*, and all I had to do was to fill in a printed outline of a tiger with coloured crayons – and I won! From small beginnings. . .

We lived in Totteridge all through the war, and war was just madly exciting for nine-year-old boys. We were far too young to realise that people were killing each other. It was fun having bombs dropped on us and having all our windows blown out. I am certain that these feelings engendered my enthusiasm for painting great events of World War II for the Services, so much later.

I remember such funny things that happened during the war. Realising what Hitler's *Luftwaffe* might do to the Shepherd family, my father commissioned a local builder to construct an air-raid shelter. He had obviously never built one before because it had only been completed a few weeks when my brother and I, playing on top of it, went through the roof!

We kept lots of goats at this time and they came in

My first attempt at art – all I had to do was colour it in!

tremendously useful as a source of milk, although we never drank a drop of the stuff. I remember spending seemingly endless hours turning handles on primitive butter-making machines while the air raids were going on, but we never ate any of the butter either. We used to queue up like all good English people did during the war, waiting our turn to get a piece of fish from the local fish-monger. As we got to the top of the queue and were told, 'sorry love, no more fish', we would surreptitiously pass him a pat of goat's butter under the counter and, in return, would get the odd kipper or piece of fresh haddock. Of course it was a bit naughty, but everyone seemed to be doing that sort of thing to survive.

A few months before Christmas, we used to buy day-old turkey chicks for fattening for the Christmas meal, but when the day came, the whole family would sit in silence around the Christmas lunch table mourning the end of 'Grandpa Turks' – after all, by then he had become a member of the family. All through the months leading up to Christmas, in the worst of the air raids, we would bring him and his chums into the kitchen at night for 'safety'. Why on earth we thought that, had the house received a direct hit, the turkeys would be safer in the kitchen than out in the garden, I can't imagine.

School Days

Going to school every day on the 251 bus (it still runs on that route) was so often filled with excitement. The bus used to stop when the fighting overhead got really bad. We would leap out to watch the vapour trails in the sky and hear the chatter of machine-gun fire as Hurricane and Spitfire fought Dornier, Heinkel and ME 109.

My brother and I must have been something of a menace to the authorities. With Dad away in the war, our mother had long since given up any attempt to keep us down in the shelter at night when something exciting was happening overhead; we insisted on running up in our pyjamas to watch. On one particularly bad night, a whole load of incendiary bombs was dropped in the field next door to us. We watched them come down and, at first light, before the police arrived on the scene, we spent a dangerous but blissfully happy hour, picking up all the tails and one partially unexploded bomb from the hole it had made – I still have it in our attic. We used the tails as flower vases!

At school, war was the great topic of conversation. We would swap souvenirs – pieces of land mine, parachute and bits of crashed German aeroplane. German aeroplanes were falling like autumn leaves over the southern half of England at this time and those that were not too bent were put on display in local town and village centres to raise money for 'Spitfire Week'. I remember queuing up along with all the snotty-nosed little schoolboys to sit in the cockpits. We were only allocated a certain amount of time each and the event was 'supervised' by an old bloke in the Home Guard who must have been at least 85 and was fast asleep anyway. By the time the last boy had climbed down the ladder on the far side of the aeroplane we had, between us, done far more damage to it than the RAF did shooting it down; everything removable ended up under our bulging shirts and jerseys.

When it was time to leave prep school, Father sent me to Stowe School in the unspoiled wilds of Buckinghamshire. I can only assume that he decided to send me there on the rather strange assumption that Hitler's *Luftwaffe* would never fly north of Watford. They did, and Stowe was bombed soon after my arrival.

To anyone who knows it, Stowe must surely be one of the most beautiful places in England, with its hundreds of acres of magnificent trees, sweeping lawns, vast lakes and temples. Its beauty was bound to brush off on anyone with even the most minimal of artistic inclinations. It certainly shaped my future far more than I realised at the time. Art, for me, was born at Stowe, but for the wrong reasons; it was just that anything was better than the torture of playing rugby. I used to invent every possible excuse to get into the art school where life was altogether gentler. Painting, for which I had no particular enthusiasm and certainly no talent, was infinitely preferable to being squashed under a heap of writhing bodies in a sea of mud, risking every bone in my body in what was apparently a game – I could not quite see the point of it.

The art school at Stowe was rather like a club, where the most artistic among us donned yellow waistcoats and went faintly Bohemian on Thursday afternoons. It was here that I did my very first oil painting. It was a monstrosity of birds, on a piece of cardboard. I still have it all these years later. It is one of my most treasured possessions because not only does it reduce anyone seeing it into uncontrolled hysterics, but it proves, as I have just said, that I had no talent.

Musically speaking, Stowe was a marvellous place and I spent a good deal of time involved in this aspect of life; I never really bothered about horrible things like mathematics and science. Towards the end of my time at Stowe I had the honour of being secretary of the Music Society. It was undoubtedly this initiation which has developed over the years into a passion for all kinds of music. For example, I love Mahler's great romantic symphonies and the nostalgia of Glenn Miller and can easily switch from Mahler to Count Basie and back again. I hate painting in silence so I have the music on full blast while I work. (I met Count Basie once. I would love to have met Mahler!)

In those days, Stowe had the most marvellous music master who used to pay out of his own pocket for world-class orchestras and soloists to come down to give recitals at the school. The only venue at the time was the old gymnasium which had been built as a temporary structure in 1923, but was still there. On one occasion, I had the embarrassing task of smoothing the ruffled feathers of the great Beno Moiseiwitsch, of international fame, who was to give a piano recital in the gym. Heaven knows what he must have thought of the rope ladders dangling over his head as he played.

AN INAUSPICIOUS START

LUCK PLAYS a part, I believe, in anyone's success and I am certain that I have had more than my fair share of it. However, in the formative years of my life the indications were that I was not going to have much success in anything. In fact, my early life was a series of disasters.

Kenya

At the age of 19, I left Stowe and had to think of earning some sort of a living. As a child my ambition was to be a game warden in Africa – nothing else mattered. This unlikely desire must have been born in me simply because of my obsession with books on Africa, which I would collect and read avidly. A number of these books, some of which I still have, were written by the big game hunters who went to Africa in the early part of the century. These were people who seemed to shoot everything that moved in the name of 'sport'. It is interesting to re-read these books. Now that I have opened my eyes and have learned a great deal about what we are doing to our wildlife and to our world, I have to say that they leave me with feelings of revulsion and disgust. No wonder there is so little wildlife left now. However, reading them as an impressionable small boy, they simply gave me the romantic idea that it would be fun and exciting to be out in the sun all day, wearing short pants, a hat with a leopard skin round the brim, and 'looking after the animals', as portrayed in some of those awful early Hollywood films. I was going to be a game warden; I had absolutely no qualifications, I had never even been abroad, except on a day trip to Calais – hardly a qualification to be a Kenyan game warden. But I was certainly arrogant; I thought I was God's gift to the Kenya National Parks!

My dad did nothing to discourage me from being a game warden in Africa, adopting the philosophy that, if that was what I wanted to be, he would not stand in my way. Our family had some vague sort of a link with someone in Kenya – apparently an uncle of mine knew a coffee farmer and he had been told about me. For some reason, he had generously decided to take me under his wing. Nobody asked me if I was interested in coffee farming: I wasn't; I was going to be a game warden.

In January 1950, my father and I drove down to Southampton and I boarded a BOAC flying boat which, in those days, flew a regular service, via various pieces of water, all the way down to South Africa. It was the first time I had ever flown and I was excited beyond measure at the fact that I was at last journeying to far-off places to achieve my ambition. It never occurred to me that there might be any pitfalls. Even the flight should have been fun, but in those days the aeroplanes flew through the heavy clouds instead of above them. Not helped by the fact that the man opposite me seemed to be eating pork chops all the way from Southampton to Lake Naivasha in Kenya, I was violently sick for the whole 36-hour journey. So I looked like death when I arrived and felt even worse!

The first night was spent on my own in a hotel on the lakeside and, although perhaps I didn't realise it at the time, the magic of Africa was beginning to brush off on me – in spite of the fact that I was feeling so ghastly.

The next morning, Frank Crawford, the coffee farmer, met me and drove me up to his farm near Lake Victoria. I soon began to realise that I was going to be a very square peg in a very round hole. Frank was a fairly hard man, but I was totally useless to him, and he very quickly told me so, in no uncertain terms. I was miserable. Up until then, the thought of homesickness had never occurred to me, but within 12 hours of arriving at the farm it hit me. I had no mobility and felt imprisoned. Where were all the lions and elephants? There were none around the farm.

I at once wrote hysterical letters to my dad, pleading to come home, and then counted the minutes until the replies came; I almost made myself ill with unhappiness. In the meantime, my baggage arrived. I had left England fully prepared to spend five years in Kenya and I am now filled with horror and shame at the thought of what it cost my father to fly out all my worldly possessions. While Frank looked on, the enormous crate was off-loaded from the truck. I had brought my bicycle with me; it hadn't occurred to either my father or myself that there were quite a few bicycles in Africa! I had even packed a moth-eaten old lion skin which I had bought for £1 in a junk shop in Buckingham when I was at Stowe – and they do have lions in Africa, too!

After a month on the coffee farm, at which point I am quite certain that Frank was only too delighted to get rid of me, I finally left and went to Nairobi. I believed that all I had to do was to knock on the door of the head game warden's office and say, 'Here I am, I have come to be a game warden,' and he would reply, 'How wonderful David, welcome to the Kenya National Parks.' He didn't. My world was in ruins. However, I did meet some wonderful people on my visit. On one occasion I was taken down to Amboseli by one of the game wardens and shown my very first herd of elephants in front of Mount Kilimanjaro. I didn't realise it at that moment, but my life would never be quite the same again.

Meanwhile my father, in response to my even more frantic pleas to come home, said, quite rightly, that as he had paid my airfare out to Kenya, I would have to stay and earn my own passage back to England. I realised that he was right, and it was a shock, but I was gradually growing up and becoming slightly less insufferable.

I happened to be reading the *East African Standard* and I saw an advertisement for a receptionist in a hotel at Malindi, on the Kenyan coast. I knew nothing about 'recepting', but, incredibly, I applied and got the job. I was paid £1 a week, which I have since been told was a lousy deal – for the hotel! However, Peter and Polly Mumford, who owned the Sinbad Hotel, were absolutely marvellous to me from the moment I arrived. In fact, even before I had unpacked my suitcase, they gave me a pair of goggles and said, 'Take this party of Americans out goggle fishing.' I didn't even know what goggle fishing meant, but I impressed the Americans; I am sure they felt that I had lived in Kenya all my life.

It would obviously take some time to pay my passage home on earnings of £1 a week, so I decided to turn to my quite remarkable lack of painting talent and paint some more ghastly pictures of birds flying over the fens. (I had to paint on plasterboard, the only material I could find as the nearest art store was in Nairobi.) I must have seemed pretty stupid painting such subjects sitting under a palm tree on a sun-drenched beach by the Indian Ocean, but I suppose that it was no more stupid than painting elephants in Cornwall. Anyway, I sold seven of these horrors at £10 each to the gullible, or culture-starved (or both) public of Malindi. The pictures paid my passage home on a Union Castle Steamer.

Buses or Art?

Once home I had two choices in front of me: to work as a bus driver or to starve as an artist. Intellectually, I was

My first oil painting. No wonder I was thrown out of art college.

anything but bright and driving buses was probably the only thing I thought I could do to earn a steady living. The other prospect, starving as an artist, I put like that because I thought at that time that all artists had to starve. (The sad thing is that some people still think that to be an artist, you must live in a garret with a mistress and go Bohemian, cutting your ear off like poor old Van Gogh did.)

So I made the great decision that I would be an artist. We had only heard of one art school – the Slade School of Fine Art in London. I applied to go there. As an entrance examination, I had to show my work, my one picture, the ghastly painting of birds on plasterboard. They took one look at it and decided that I was not worth teaching; they told me to go and drive a bus.

Actually, that is not exactly what they said. Very many years later, when I was being interviewed about my life on a BBC radio programme, the researcher decided to ring up the Slade to ask if they still had the rejection notice for me. He was incredulous when they said they had; they obviously don't empty their wastepaper baskets very often. To my amusement and, no doubt, that of the listeners, it was read out over the radio. The Slade School of Fine Art obviously had a sense of humour because they described the bird painting thus: 'David Shepherd entered a painting of birds of dubious ancestry, flying in anatomically impossible positions, over a lavatorial green sea.' What a perfect description.

I had failed to become a game warden. Now I had failed to become an artist. It looked like the buses!

GETTING ON COURSE

I REALLY DO BELIEVE in miracles. I was just on the point of getting a job with the local bus company, driving buses around the Surrey countryside, when I happened to be invited to a cocktail party in London. I don't really like going to parties where I don't know anyone, but this one changed my life. I was introduced to a professional artist called Robin Goodwin. I had never heard of him, he had certainly never heard of me. I told him about my disastrous life, failing to become a game warden and then being rejected by art school. It didn't help my sagging morale when he said, 'Well, I am not going to teach you, David. I don't teach anybody. I don't have the time.' However, he did offer to look at my bird picture if I was prepared to drive to his studio in Chelsea the following morning.

I arrived there next morning, he took one look at the ghastly thing and said, 'Do you want me to teach you?' It was as simple as that. After all these years, I can only guess that he took me on as a challenge, or was it pity? To the end of my days, I will never know.

The first day with Robin was traumatic. He said, 'I am going to tell you a few basic things now and if you are not prepared to accept them, you can get out of my studio for good. First of all, just because you think you are artistic and the world owes you a living, don't imagine you are different from anybody else, you are not. An artist, or a pianist, is no different from a farmer or an electrician. You are going to be working seven days a week in your studio, using every hour of daylight that God gives you, including Sundays. You have got to be there at nine o'clock in the morning in November when it is so dark you can't see the canvas and paint to pay the bills.' Piling on the agony, he continued, 'I am never going to say anything good about anything you do for the next three years because I am going to assume that you know the good things. I am only going to tell you the bad things.' I felt like bursting into tears. All my illusions about being an artist had been shattered in one blow.

When this short sharp session of verbal torture was over, Robin said, 'I've got a commission to paint Westminster Bridge; come on, you're coming with me.' We both hopped on a bus. Robin had his easel, covered in paint from years of hard work; I had my shiny brand new one. We alighted and, within a matter of minutes, Robin

was painting away quite happily right by the bus stop, completely oblivious to the crowds around him. I was paralysed with fear. I had never even painted in the middle of a field; here I was in the middle of London. I tried to pretend that it was a better composition down the steps, behind the wall, in front of County Hall. In fact down there I couldn't see anything anyway, and, of course, Robin saw through this straightaway. 'Come on up here and paint beside me.'

For the first three days, I don't think I touched the brush onto the canvas. Every time a bus went by, every few seconds, about thirty people craned their necks to see what we were doing. But this was good discipline and would enable me to paint in almost impossible conditions in later years.

Robin was primarily a marine and portrait painter. During the years that I was with him, he undertook a large number of portrait commissions and I painted these alongside him. I also experienced just how hard such painting is from the sitter's point of view.

One commission Robin had was to paint the portrait of the chancellor of a university; unfortunately the man had just died and so the face had to be done from photographs. I, being the student, had to sit for the body! I learnt then just how important it is to sit absolutely still. I was dressed in silk robes, which did not make my life any easier. Robin reminded me that every time I moved my arm all the folds in the silk would be different when I put it down again, so I couldn't scratch. But, as he pointed out, it was 'all part of your training'. If you see the painting, you are looking at my body – not many people know that!

Specialising in portraits, it was inevitable that Robin was asked to paint a number of debutantes – feats of sheer endurance, I cannot understand how he managed to stand the mental anguish. The girls came along at ten in the morning, dolled up in their best evening gowns and covered in makeup. Many of them had faces that seemed rather like pudgy puddings and some were accompanied by Mummy to make sure that we behaved ourselves. (I reckoned that it was a very small risk to the girls concerned – with faces like puddings at ten in the morning, there was very little incentive to do anything but paint!) Sometimes, 'Mummy' would say to Robin,

'Make Angela prettier than she really is, won't you?' If Mummy then left, Robin used to say, 'Go behind that screen, take off all that makeup, let your hair down, put this polo-neck sweater on, and then I'll paint you.'

The Streets of London

They were wonderfully happy, hilarious days, painting with Robin out on the streets of London, but they had their problems too. Even on a Sunday, we were often such an attraction that we would have one or two hundred people standing behind us – some actually in front of us so that we could not see what we were trying to paint – and, on occasions, we were offered fatuous and stupid advice on how to do it. 'I wouldn't do it like that in my art class,' was one comment. The girl who said this as she brushed by looked, I imagined, exactly like the paintings that she created at her art college – chair legs and torn up cornflake packets nailed on to bits of plywood. People would sometimes stand so close behind us that we could smell the peppermints they breathed down the back of our necks. We always had a way of dealing with those who really wouldn't get out of our way – a quick step back, flourishing a paint-covered palette, worked wonders. Both of us must be on miles of movie film because tourists with cine cameras often took us to be part of London's famous landmarks.

Crowds did become exceedingly tiresome at times. Although we were not causing the obstruction, there were times when we had to be moved on, because of the number of people watching us. It was heartbreaking, just as one was 'getting into' the painting.

On just a few other occasions, we fell foul of the law. Robin and I discovered that from somewhere in the dim and distant past there was a law which said that if your easel had three legs you had to have a permit, if it had two legs, you didn't; presumably with only two legs, it falls over anyway! One day, we were approached by a young policeman who was obviously rather too keen to impress us with his knowledge of legal matters. 'Have you got a permit to do that?' he asked, slightly officiously. We both knew how to cope with the situation. The policeman, like so many others, obviously had the idea that all artists are pretty crazy 'up top' and we played on this supposition.

Robin and I dropped our lower jaws and adopted a completely vacant expression without issuing any audible sound at all. It worked like magic. The policeman, obviously thinking that we were completely mad, walked on – and we continued painting.

I was a bit arrogant, even in those days. One particular sunny Sunday morning when I was painting in London, a very large saloon drove up and stopped in the road beside me. Two extremely glamorous models got out, dressed in their evening gowns, followed by a gentleman with several cameras round his neck who was obviously a fashion photographer. He proceeded to twist and turn the girls into ludicrous and impossibly anatomical positions on the traffic island for his photograph, which was no doubt destined to appear in *Harper's* or *Vogue*. I suddenly realised that I was going to be a blur in the background. I had no intention of being a blur in anyone's photograph and asked him to go somewhere else – I obviously already had very big ideas!

We certainly 'made our mark' on the streets of London. On one occasion, at the commencement of a day's work, my palette fell face downwards and, when I picked it up, there were fourteen little coloured pyramids on the pavement. Inevitably, during the course of the day, our watching public walked through these little piles of paint. Coloured footmarks went off in all directions; they are probably still there.

In the middle of winter in the London Docks, it was often so cold that by the end of the day, we found it almost impossible to fold up our easels. On one occasion, one of Robin's paintings was caught in the wind, blown right off the easel, and the last he saw of it was floating down towards Greenwich.

We painted many pictures on the Chelsea Embankment looking towards Battersea Power Station. Painting the lovely old Victorian lamps on the Embankment wall required a lot of concentration and careful work, often ruined in a matter of seconds when a bus rushed by a few feet behind us, creating a dust storm and covering the painting with a layer of grit from the pavement – or when a fat fly landed right in the middle of a freshly painted piece of sky, then dragged its feet all over the picture's most detailed parts. Back at the studio hours would be spent picking all the bits of muck from the wet paint with a palette knife. On one occasion, we were obviously being watched from a window opposite. The first thing we knew about it was a lady brushing past and saying, 'When you have finished with it, leave it under the seat.' We looked around, and there was a basket beautifully packed with a cold lunch, complete with knives and forks, and a thermos flask of scalding hot tea. We never did find

Westminster Square, 1952. I couldn't do this now because of the traffic.

13

out who she was, but she obviously thought we were starving – a very kind lady indeed.

Robin was a very practical man. He told me that he was not going to 'waste' time teaching me history of art. 'You can learn all that stuff by getting a book out of the local library. In any case, learning when Botticelli painted all those fat naked women is not going to help you pay your bills.' He was quite marvellous at knowing just how far to go without breaking my spirit. Several times, in a screaming temper, I was on my way down the stairs to my car parked outside, all ready to pack it in for good and go home. On one of the more emotional of these occasions he leaned out of the window and shouted down at me, 'Come on back, you silly little blighter, I am still teaching you, so you must be worth teaching.' That was, as far as I remember, the only kind thing that he said in three years; but it made sense. It was no good telling me that everything I did was good, which it wasn't, because I would have learnt nothing.

The Open Air Show on Thames Embankment

We both knew that there was no better way to get work seen than to get it into an exhibition. For many years, one of the best showcases for any artist has been the open air 'free for all' art exhibition on the Thames Embankment during the first few weeks in May. The whole idea of mixing up a complete cross section of the amateur and professional art scene and putting it in front of the public must be a good one. I believe there is scarcely any more productive or enjoyable way of exhibiting than hanging paintings on railings in public places – indeed, the idea seems to have spread because many lengths of railings in London now have paintings hanging on them on Sundays. The marvellous thing about the Thames Embankment show is the hotch-potch of so many different sorts of painters and paintings. Painters of completely different social and financial backgrounds mix happily together. A large length of chain-link fencing is put up along the edge of the path in the gardens and this is sub-divided with tapes in sections of approximately two metres (6ft) square. When I was exhibiting on the Embankment, we would arrive the night before and, when Big Ben struck midnight, we would put a picture up and claim a pitch. We could then go away and risk the painting being stolen which, oddly enough, it never was – or else stay there until the early hours. Each pitch was provided with a tarpaulin on the back of the fence so that when it rained, this could be pulled over the pictures. The whole thing cost the artist absolutely nothing.

There were always more artists than pitches available

Victoria Embankment Gardens, 1956; my first exposure to the public. (E. Millington)

and at the end of each day we balloted for the next day. We never knew where our pitch was going to be and we would always be next to somebody new. The great thing about this exhibition, quite apart from the fact that there was no selection committee or hanging fee, was the wonderful freedom. You could put one small picture in the middle of your pitch or cover the entire area with miniatures. You could come and go as you pleased, sell for whatever prices you thought reasonable and the public loved it. Enormous crowds of people would come through in the lunch hour every day, particularly in warm sunny weather. Besides, being on the Embankment, you never knew who was going to come out of the Savoy Hotel!

The sense of comradeship between us all was a side of artistic life that I have only ever experienced on these occasions. The traditional ones among us, those who paint something recognisable, are chasms apart from the Bohemian types who fire paint out of a gun and ride their bicycles over their pictures, but we all got on famously with each other. I used to sit on the seat opposite my pitch in all weathers and if I had not sold much and was thirsty or hungry, I asked whoever was next to me to look after my pictures while I went into Bert's café under Charing Cross bridge. I would always do the same for the artist next to me.

Unfortunately the sensational press used to come down to the show every year and write a lot of rubbish about 'Bohemia among the tulips'. This, and other sickening clichés about starving artists, used to appear in the evening papers. One day I was sitting opposite my pitch in the sunshine, wearing my Stowe school tie. Another 'old boy', walking through the exhibition in his lunch hour from his city office, complete with bowler and pinstripe suit, looked aghast to see me apparently on my 'beam ends'. I have never seen such a pompous expression on anyone's face; he obviously thought that I was letting down the school. However, his attitude changed after he had heard of my sales of the previous days. 'Good grief, you lucky blighter, I can't earn that in three months in my stuffy office!'

Fashions used to change in the open air art exhibition. One year it might be flower pictures, and then landscapes. I remember one artist who 'caught on' to such an extent that he was busy wrapping pictures up all day like a barrow boy in Oxford Street; then he would dash home and paint a whole lot more for the next day. Two elderly ladies came every year and used to paint hundreds of pictures especially for the exhibition. They came up at the beginning of May and established themselves in a comfortable hotel. Their pitch was completely covered in little flower pictures, never much more than 15 x 10cm (6 x 4in). For five shillings you got two flowers in a pot, and for two and sixpence you got one. They sold like hot cakes, enabling the ladies to live comfortably in Hove while they painted another lot during the remaining eleven months of the year.

There were several professional artists like myself who recognised the Embankment as a marvellous showcase. Indeed, people used to come down from the opening of the Royal Academy Summer Exhibition, which took place at roughly the same time, and say what a breath of fresh air it was to see some real painting at last.

It was from the open air art exhibition of the first year that I sold my very first picture – and learned a lesson at the same time. It was a small English landscape priced at twenty-five pounds. A smartly dressed gentleman walked through the gardens, saw my picture, and offered me twelve pounds for it. He obviously thought that I was looking fed up – which I was. He beat me down pound by pound until I gave in. I then carried the painting along to his car, he handed the painting over to his chauffeur and was driven off in his Rolls Royce. I swore that I would never be beaten down in that fashion again. (I am, quite often, but only when it's with friends, and then it's fun.)

'Never Let a Painting Beat You'

One of the many things that I shall always remember Robin telling me is 'Never let a painting beat you'. Painting, like composing, is a very lonely job. The artist has no one to turn to and is solely responsible for the failure or the success of whatever he is working on. I, like many other artists, I am sure, have often had to fight a picture to make sure that it turns out to the best of my ability. If it goes wrong and I chuck it away and start another one, it's a waste of time, effort, and paint. That is why I have only one disastrous painting in my attic! I had started a major canvas of three lions, a big male in the centre, and a female on either side. It was so ghastly that I knew it would never work. Many months after I had rejected it, a very persuasive American friend who had already purchased a number of my pictures, came to dinner. 'Have you anything I can actually take away with

me tonight?' I pointed out that there was, even in those days, a waiting list of some years, but I remembered my lions. Both of us went up into the attic and I put the painting on the floor. 'It's ghastly,' I said. 'Why don't you just cut out the centre lion, he's super?', my friend asked. I thought for a moment. He was right. I got a razor blade and cut through the canvas right around the lion's head. He paid me on the spot and took it back to America with him, beaming with pleasure. I now have a large canvas of two female lions, with a hole in the middle!

At the Royal Academy

Robin not only taught me how to paint, he also had some pretty strong ideas about 'the art establishment', critics, and 'modern art'. It was in 1954 that I sent in a painting to the Royal Academy for their Summer Exhibition and, by sheer chance rather than merit, it was accepted. An impossibly large number of paintings are sent in to this show every year and I believe that it is physically impossible for a committee to sit for more than a week with a continuous stream of paintings going past them and still make selections. Occasionally, I reckon, an academician opens one eye, lifts a hand, and the painting is accepted; then everybody goes to sleep again. However, it was a prestigious thing to be accepted – my picture was of a little antique shop, and it was number 648 in the catalogue. It was hung above an electric plug socket almost at floor level, in gallery heaven-knows-what-number.

My mother and father were, not unnaturally, proud that I had a picture hanging. My father put his best suit on, which was always a bit of an effort, and we went to the private view. We walked up the steps of Burlington House and the commissionaire's arm came down across my father's chest preventing him from entering. 'Haven't you read your ticket?' he said, rather aggressively, 'It does in fact say "Admit two, including exhibitor".' I went down to the office for another ticket and this was refused, so I had to take my mother round the exhibition, put her into a 'crawling position' to see my picture and then leave her out in the car park while my father went in. This was bad enough but the thing that really annoyed me was that so many of the people drinking champagne in front of our pictures at the private view were celebrities who had nothing whatsoever to do with painting – for example, film starlets being photographed by the press in the hope of getting a star part; to them it was just a social event at the beginning of the London season. This kind of sham façade gives painting exhibitions, particularly this one, a bad name, which I think is a pity.

I also believe that the Royal Academy should move with

the times far more; if they have to exhibit door knobs, chair legs and torn up cornflakes packets, they should also realise that the public want to see realism by 'popular' artists as well. Of course it's a free country and every artist can paint what and how he pleases. However, I believe it is now a sad reflection on this modern age that we have to put up with some misguided idiot with too much money and no taste buying a sheep's head preserved in formaldehyde for £20,000. What do the British public really think when they go into the Tate Gallery and see seven tons of rice spread all over the floor? I know what they think because they tell me. The vast majority of people like to recognise what they are looking at. I believe the 'art establishment' has gone completely mad. Traditional, representational painting is not going to be swept aside because a few rather strange people start throwing paint at the wall. (Those guys who painted those wonderful drawings of wild animals on cave walls thousands of years before Christ did it properly!) That's what I think, anyway.

On My Own

I am certainly glad that I went to that cocktail party and met Robin Goodwin. After the three most momentous and character-forming years of my life, he finally said, 'David, you are on your own, I can't teach you any more.'

I shall be grateful to him for the rest of my life for that training and for instilling discipline into me, because it is discipline that it's all about.

With Robin Goodwin. If I hadn't met him I wouldn't be writing this book.

Just after I had finished my training with Robin, I had my very first one-man exhibition in London, and Sir Miles Thomas, the chairman of BOAC at the time, opened it for me. The show included English landscapes and railway paintings, as well as aircraft pictures; there was even a nude study, a picture that I had done as an exercise with Robin. The chairman of one of our major industries asked to see it and he immediately loved it – he went dashing into the dining room with it and hung it on his wall, but his wife said, 'Darling, we cannot possibly eat our dinner with that on the wall.' (It was rather a nice little study actually, although I say it myself, and it only showed the girl's back!)

I was delighted when a camera team for Pathé Pictorial came to the exhibition to film the paintings. They put the appropriate soundtrack behind the pictures and it was quite remarkable how they came alive in the process. I remember one particular painting that worked especially well. I had painted, from life, a portrait of a Lancaster Bomber sitting in the sunshine at Blackbushe Airport shortly before being flown off to the scrapyard. The

Painting at Heathrow, 1953.

camera team zoomed in to each of the four Merlin engines to create the illusion of them running at full power and one could almost see the aircraft coming out of the canvas. Pathé Pictorial No 48 was shown in cinemas all over the country; the first real burst of Shepherd publicity!

Planes and my First Successes

Luck still continued to play its part. When I left Robin, my parents allowed me to stay at home for a full year. I therefore did not have to earn my living immediately. However well I might have been trained, my work was obviously immature and had I had to support myself from the beginning, I might well have suffered through the necessity of my having to take every sort of commission that came my way. Instead of this, I was shielded by my parents' generosity, and I was able to spend the whole of that twelve months at the then London Airport, now Heathrow. I had always been fascinated by aircraft, ever since being a small boy and living through the blitz. It seemed natural, therefore, that I would specialise in aviation painting, and Heathrow was just up the road.

London Airport was not the concrete jungle that it is today. I had a permit which enabled me to paint almost anywhere I liked and I painted some twenty pictures in the long hot summer of 1953. If the conditions in London were bad, they were worse at Heathrow. I invariably had to weigh down the easel with bricks, to stop the whole thing taking off in the perpetual gale that seemed to be blowing. However, there were plenty of subjects – lovely old aeroplanes like Stratocruisers and Viscounts – 'planes with propellers'. Setting my easel up in front of my subjects, I even became known as the 'London Airport Artist'. Many coach parties were taken around the airport to see the 'sights', and I was one of them.

One particular painting illustrates how friendly Heathrow was. I set my easel up in front of a super Constellation – a beautiful four-engined airliner, which belonged to Trans-Canada Airlines. There seemed to be no sign of life around it so there was no particular hurry. I had spent three and a half days painting all the meticulous detail of the aeroplane in front of me and I had about three more hours to complete the picture when, activity at last, a couple of guys got into the cockpit and opened the window. They shouted at me, 'Sorry mate, we are going to Toronto.' (I felt like saying 'about time too!') Seeing the ruination of the painting by the immediate departure of my subject, and having the 'cheek of old Harry', I brazenly shouted up at them, 'If you take the plane away now, it will ruin my painting. Please, can I have another three hours?' Far from the expected response, 'Sorry mate, tough', they replied, 'OK, we'll come back in three hours!' Life was a great deal easier and slower in those days.

By hanging my paintings, such as they were, in the public enclosure at London Airport, I was gradually getting noticed by the people who mattered, such as the chairman of BOAC at that time. He arranged for me to go on a test flight in a Comet to 'see what cloudscapes really looked like at 35,000ft'. I was also giving paintings of Viscounts and Comets away, as I realised that this was probably the only chance of having my work hanging in the boardrooms of the big aviation companies. I believe that eventually they got so fed up with me that they felt obliged to commission the odd one, and I gather that they still have those paintings, at £20 a time. The rest are in my attic, but I suppose that they do at least represent a small piece of aviation history.

By now, I had got myself married and we were starting a young family so I had commitments. I was adequately, but only just, earning my living painting aeroplanes and English landscapes. I had met my wife Avril when I was living in Camberley, where she worked in a bank. Shortly after this, she landed herself a much more stimulating job. At this time, Capital Airlines of Washington had ordered seventy-five Viscount Airliners from Vickers and they were assembled at Hurn Airport. She became private secretary to the Capital Airlines' representative who was overseeing the final completion and delivery of the brand new aeroplanes to the United States. One amusing aspect of this was a result of the way the aircraft were prepared for export. They were stripped completely inside with just a few seats – the rest would be fitted later on arrival in America. The American ferry crews would come over to collect them and, prior to departure, would go around the antique shops in Bournemouth buying Victorian lamp standards and huge great Victorian dressers, which would then be loaded into the aeroplanes. Consequently, when I was offered a free lift in one of the Viscounts, I was accompanied by vast quantities of our historical past. It was an interesting trip as we flew via Iceland and Greenland, finally arriving in Washington where, ostensibly, I was destined to paint commissions for the boardrooms of Boeing in Seattle and Douglas in Los Angeles, but it never worked out. That is another story, and I came home on the SS United States, temporarily almost penniless. However, that was not Avril's fault!

THE BIG BREAK

THE ROYAL AIR FORCE was slowly beginning to recognise my work and the occasional commission was coming my way. However, it was in 1960 that the big break came – that year was the catalyst in my life. In the early part of the year, a very official-looking letter, with some important initials on the envelope, dropped through my letter box. It was marked, 'C-in-C, BFAP'. I knew what commander-in-chief meant. Was I really becoming noticed by the top people? I hadn't a clue what BFAP meant until I opened the letter. In fact, it was an invitation from the Commander-in-Chief, British Forces Arabian Peninsula, inviting me out to Aden to paint as a guest of the Royal Air Force. He happened to have seen an article featuring my aircraft pictures in colour in a company magazine and had said to his ADC, 'I wonder if this chap might come out to Aden and paint for us?'

Reading on, I realised that there was no guarantee of any commissioned work. The Commander-in-Chief would simply arrange for me to be given a free seat on a Royal Air Force 216 Squadron Comet when it happened to be flying from RAF Lyneham down the route to Australia, via Aden. When I arrived, I would be shown around the whole area and the rest would be up to me. I had only vaguely heard of Aden, as a rather hot and smelly place at the southern end of the Red Sea, but it seemed very exciting. Little did I imagine what would transpire.

Aden

On arrival in Aden I was met with the usual RAF hospitality. In fact, I have never felt so important in my life. I was even driven around Aden in a car with a flag on the front, but I have to say that was only when the Air Officer Commanding was with me in the car! Nevertheless, it was rather nice to have breakfast brought to me in bed by his batman. I have never had a batman before – one with white gloves on, too!

I started my tour around the many squadrons based in Aden, showing them photographs of my work, together with various sketches. The reaction was totally apathetic and I soon realised why. Apparently a certain lady artist had visited the Royal Air Force in Aden just before I arrived, and she had made such a nuisance of herself that they had been frightened of any 'artists' ever coming in their direction again. A couple of nights later, I attended a rather posh dinner party at which a large number of very senior officers from all three services were present, and there it was decided that Shepherd would be flown home again in the first Comet that came from Australia en route to England. I took it philosophically. After all, I had had a very relaxing few days and met a lot of wonderful people; the aeroplanes were flying anyway so I had not cost the taxpayer anything. It happened, however, that no Royal Air Force Comet was due for over a week so, rather than sit on my backside and do nothing, I decided to explore. I had been told of a place called Slave Island where dhows, the Arab fishing vessels that sailed the spice routes of old, were still being built in almost exactly the same way as they had been in the days of the Bible. I happened to have a blank canvas with me, and that canvas changed my life.

Just occasionally in his creative lifetime, an artist may paint a picture that he feels is rather special, either because of its quality, or for some other reason. I have painted some three thousand paintings in my career so far but *Slave Island* must be a major landmark if only because of all the things that led from it.

I spent several days on Slave Island and painted the whole picture on the spot. When it was completed, I showed it to the Commander-in-Chief. He said, 'That's a hell of a lot better than the sketches and photographs that you were showing us, let's have a party.' We hung the painting up on the wall and I obtained forty-eight commissions that evening. Now it seemed that everyone in Aden wanted my work. I was commissioned by Shell, BP, Aden Airways, a large number of Arab traders, all three services and various shipping lines.

The 'Radfan'

The Commander-in-Chief RAF said, 'Look, you don't have to go straight back to England, do you? Would you like to see more of our sphere of operations?' And so it was that I spent a hectic and exciting six weeks flying with the Royal Air Force in every conceivable type of aircraft.

Every day, we would fly up into the 'Radfan', an area of arid mountains looking more like the moon than anywhere earthly. Up on top of the escarpment that ran all along the coast, little encampments had been set up by British troops to keep the various warring factions of Arab tribesmen apart; as usual, the British were in the middle! The troops were stationed under canvas at various little mud-brick villages, places that had not changed since the days of the Bible. Most of these camps were virtually cut off from the outside world except for the help provided by the Royal Air Force. How the aircraft, the Beverleys, and other types, flew at all, I cannot imagine. The conditions were appalling. Aden airfield itself was built on salt and, together with the high humidity, the corrosion problems must have been monumental, but the Royal Air Force 'kept them flying'. At the villages themselves, the only concession to modern living for the Arabs who lived there was the fact that the 'big white bird' would fly in and land on its own dust storm on the airstrip to deliver supplies.

I had a love affair with the Beverley. Was the thing really meant to fly? The first time I ever saw that monumental elephantine and much-loved transport aircraft was at the Farnborough Air Show, highly polished and surrounded by geraniums. Here, it was a different story; it is a very strange feeling to be able to sit in the cab of a three-ton Bedford truck, when one is 1,200 metres (4,000ft) up in the air. If I was bored, I could go for a cross-country run. These amazing aeroplanes carried trucks in their hold and thirty or forty troops up in the tail.

Since the demise of the Beverley I have often wondered how on earth the Royal Air Force have ever managed without them.

Setting up my easel in remote places such as Beihan was an experience I shall never forget. The Arabs thought I was writing a letter home when they saw me squeeze the oil paint out of the tubes. One guy got terribly upset because I was painting the palm tree in front of me. It turned out that he owned it and he thought I was going to take it away by putting it on the canvas. In this modern world of high technology it is a rare thing indeed for an artist to be able to find subjects and paint in a place like this. There are not many such places left.

One village was accessible by 'road' and I managed to cadge a lift on the 'Dhala Convoy'. This was a weekly procession of army Bedford trucks and Land Rovers, which used to struggle up through the interior and up the escarpment to reach the troops at Dhala itself. The journey up to the top was particularly hair-raising. The 'road' was simply a dirt track with a sheer drop on one side; if a vehicle broke down, it would be pushed over the edge, to avoid holding up the convoy. This was important because, to add to the fun, the tribesmen from the North Yemen, the opposing side to the British, used to roll boulders down the side of the mountain on to the convoy as it was struggling up the track. Fortunately, I missed that particular form of entertainment on the journey I made. Nevertheless, my visit resulted in a most interesting painting. I offered it to the 'Royals' who took me up with them, but they said they could not afford the £90. The Arab Federal Army in Aden then purchased it, provided I made the appropriate changes to the uniforms and vehicle numbers, and they proudly hung it up in their own Officers' Mess. However, the painting has had a rather strange fate. Just before we pulled out of Aden in 1967, when I was there for yet another visit, the Senior British Officer still in the town said, 'David, we must get that super painting of yours back. The Arabs will probably burn down their Mess when we pull out.' I protested strongly, pointing out that it was actually their property. The next thing I learnt was that the painting was hanging at Warminster in Wiltshire. It was a case, yet again, of the British stealing things that don't belong to them – the Elgin Marbles all over again!

The Wadi Hadhramaut

Subsequent to all this excitement and fun in Aden, I have often been asked to choose the most memorable part of the world that I have ever managed to visit and it is obviously an impossible question to answer. I have been lucky to have seen a very great deal of the African Continent, as well as India, and many other parts of the world; but if I really pushed, the answer has to be the Wadi Hadhramaut. When I was in Aden, so many people had told me about this area that I felt I just must see it. It was not going to be simple, however, because if the villages up in the Radfan were 'easy' to get to, this was something entirely different. The Hadhramaut is an area on the edge of the empty quarter of Arabia, scarcely written about and even less visited by Europeans, but, I was told, spectacularly beautiful.

While I was there, by sheer good fortune, the Royal Air Force was chartering a DC3 from Aden Airways to make the trip in a few days time, and I was promised a lift. The flight from Aden was hot and bumpy, but finally I saw Mukalla below us. This was the port from which one managed to journey, if one was lucky, into the Hadhramaut itself. The town was an incredible sight from the air; an ancient collection of gleaming white buildings around a bay of impossible blue, with a precipitous mountain towering up behind the town, looking rather like a cake with strawberry on the bottom layer and chocolate on top. The airstrip for Mukalla was at a place called Riyan, a few miles out of the town. The runway was simply a very stony and dusty patch, hewn out of the rocks, with an old tin shed as the reception area. It looked foreboding as we came into land, but I could not see any bits of broken aeroplane at the end of the runway, so I assumed it was safer than it looked.

The doors of the aircraft were opened and it was just like putting one's head into a very hot oven. Nevertheless, the first thing I noticed was a game of cricket going on next to the runway. Talk about mad dogs and Englishmen! Apparently, the Commanding Officer at Riyan airstrip had challenged the eight Europeans living in Mukalla to a cricket match. I only had a few precious hours in the town, but I had to wait until the match was over before there would be any transport to take me there.

Going into Mukalla seemed like going into another world. The lovely Arab buildings, primitive in the extreme, climbed up the foot of that remarkable mountain. The windows had no glass in them, just gauze shutters to keep the flies and the sun out. The central feature of the curving waterfront was the mosque. Unfortunately, here I discovered that progress had actually arrived. The faithful were no longer called to prayer by means of a megaphone from the top of the tower. It was now done with a windup gramophone. They were even beginning to put modern street lighting down the main street. Such is progress.

The only vehicles in the town were a few battered ex-army Bedford trucks and one private car. This was a very dilapidated pre-war Humber. Because it was there, an enterprising Arab shopkeeper had put up a beautifully painted sign which read 'Local Rootes Group Dealer'. I took a photograph of this and showed it to their main showroom staff in Piccadilly just for the fun of it, but they took it frightfully seriously. 'This is not one of our official accredited agents.'

I did several sketches in Mukalla which I still have. Each time, I was surrounded by hoards of Arab children, full of smiles and begging for cigarettes.

During my all-too-brief visit, I was staying at the 'Official Residency of Her Britannic Majesty's Representative to the East Aden Protectorate' – the title seemed to stretch right across the top of the notepaper. However, and perhaps more aptly, the place was affectionately known as 'Dysentery Hall'. I wasn't there long enough to discover why, but I could imagine – the plumbing was somewhat primitive. Whatever shortcomings there may have been, the Union Jack was hauled down at sunset, accompanied by an Arab bugler in immaculate white uniform. It was enough to make me cry with patriotism! I count myself highly privileged to have seen this lovely place and quite possibly to have been the first artist to have painted it.

Every possible effort was made to get me up to see the Hadhramaut itself. We had no success for the first three days and then, finally, the signal came over the air: 'Reference yours 10:20 hours yesterday, artist welcome. House available. Arab cook, American anthropologist thrown in for good measure.'

Taking my life in my hands and not really knowing what to expect I, nevertheless, could not resist the temptation. This was a chance of a lifetime. A DC3 was flying back to Aden via the Hadhramaut and so we dashed off to Mukalla's airstrip.

The aircraft flew over a lunar landscape where there was no kind of habitation or greenery. Then we saw the Wadi. It looked rather like the Grand Canyon. We flew the last few miles below the top of the Wadi's walls and dropped down onto the airstrip at Gatn.

The Wadi stretches for over 160 kilometres (100 miles), rather like a gigantic channel cut deep into the barren landscape. The floor is flat bare sand and on either side, towering to 305 metres (1,000ft), are enormous sheer walls of sandstone. Little clusters of castellated mud-brick houses are huddled together here and there to form the most picturesque villages. The air is crystal clear and there is a feeling of total peace and stillness such as I have never experienced anywhere else in the world.

For the first night, I stayed in the local political agent's house, a beautiful building, painted white inside and out for coolness. After our evening meal of goat meat, we sat on the flat roof and watched the sun going down, a sight I shall never forget. As the fiery red ball dipped lower and lower towards the horizon, the shadow of one side of the Wadi climbed up the other until, at the last moment, a brilliant gold strip was sharply edged along the top of the escarpment, then it too disappeared. I painted this from life, and had to work fast!

We sat in the cool night air, without speaking; the human voice seemed an imposition in such a setting. Then our American friend put a record of Max Bruch's violin concerto on a transistor gramophone and never have I appreciated glorious music more deeply.

The challenge was to get to Shibam itself, a mud-brick skyscraper city, known as the 'Chicago of the East'. (It was not at all like Chicago.) It was not easy because vehicles were as scarce as gold, but by sheer good fortune we managed to 'confiscate' a Land Rover belonging to the Desert Locust Control people. They were generous enough to allow us to use their vehicle for a morning and we drove as fast as we could. (It turned out that my driver had been to Torquay!)

After a few hours' drive this amazing city appeared out of the heat haze. Some of the buildings rose to thirteen or fourteen storeys high and were made entirely of mud-bricks. No Europeans lived there, there was no electricity at the time, and vehicles could not get into the town. We had to leave our Land Rover outside and walk up a great ramp and through an arched gateway. The streets leading off from the town centre were just wide enough for five people to walk abreast, but this was a dangerous practice because the toilets from the buildings consisted of pipes sticking out from the wall above, so you had, in fact, to walk in line down the middle.

I know I get excited about so many things, but Shibam really has to be the most memorable place I have ever visited and, once again, I feel privileged indeed. Things change so quickly. I am told that now, in the 1990s, there is a tarmac road going all the way up to Shibam, and there is a video shop in the middle of the town centre.

Kenya and Wildlife

Returning to Aden after all this excitement, my host, the Commander-in-Chief Royal Air Force, now said, 'Kenya is part of our command here in Aden. We are going down to Nairobi tomorrow in a Beverley. Would you like to go with us?' I hesitated because I really wanted to go back home. On the other hand, I remembered my first visit as a frustrated game warden. 'OK, I wouldn't mind a lift down to the old place to see it again,' I said.

In spite of my apparent indifference at the time, I am glad that I accepted that invitation. If I hadn't, I might not be writing this book.

In 1960, Kenya was still a British colony and the Royal Air Force was stationed at Eastleigh, just outside Nairobi. I met the Station Commander and he said, 'We heard you were coming. We would like a couple of pictures for the Officers' Mess here, but we don't want aeroplanes. We fly those things all day. Do you paint elephants?'

Up until then, the thought of painting animals had never occurred to me, I had not even painted a hamster. However, I suppose I had a mild affinity with wildlife because I had read all those awful books as a child, so I thought I would have a try and, after all, it would make a change from painting aeroplanes. I went straight into Nairobi and bought a canvas and set to work on my very first wildlife painting. It was actually of a rhino chasing a Royal Air Force aeroplane off a landing strip up country in Kenya. I sold it to Royal Air Force Eastleigh for £25, including the frame. Something else was about to happen that was to influence the rest of my life dramatically.

Having delivered my first wildlife painting, I was still in Nairobi and I had a few days to spare, because there was no Air Force flight back to Aden to enable me to go home

My first wildlife painting, which changed my life.

to England. So my wife joined me in Nairobi and we went down to the Serengeti National Park in Tanzania. We knew the game warden, and driving out with him in his Land Rover very early one morning, we saw an incredibly large number of vultures circling in the sky. He said, 'That can't just be an ordinary lion's kill. There is something very wrong over there David, and we had better go over and see.' What we found had such an impact on me that it was to change the whole pattern of my life.

We came across a water-hole that had been poisoned by poachers. We found 255 zebra lying dead on the ground and the sight was so horrific that in that single dramatic moment, I knew that I had just become a conservationist.

In Print and *Wise Old Elephant*

On my return home, my career took off rapidly. Everybody seemed to want my wildlife paintings. I had my first one-man exhibition of wildlife pictures in London in 1962 and the whole lot sold in the first twenty minutes. Things were really beginning to happen. At the same time, I was beginning to see my other work in print, starting with Christmas cards and cheap calendars; never mind, it was a way of getting my paintings seen.

And it was Christmas cards in a big way, for one of the big firms in the north of England. I did some thirty paintings for them, most of which had to be set in 1890 for a reason I never really discovered; and they all had to have the inevitable snow. The best one, *Ludgate Hill in 1890*, was, in fact, a blockbuster and after all these years still reappears in their Christmas books from time to time. I remember driving in my first little car up the old A5 road to their offices in Bradford and back in a day, long before motorways; I was charging the company £30 for each painting, and that included the copyright.

Next I moved into fine art prints which was a major step forward. I had painted a couple of pictures, *The Last Bales* and *Winter Plough* and the retail price in old English money was somewhere in the region of 10/6d each. They were tremendously successful, reprinting many times. Following on from the success of these prints, it was inevitable, perhaps, that my publishers, whom I had met for the first time when I was training with Robin at the Open Air Show on the Embankment, would ask me to 'do an elephant'. It was a brave step. The production of a fine art print is an expensive process and I doubted if enough people would buy the print to justify the expense. They certainly did. *Wise Old Elephant* took off. It was published in 1962 and lasted for 25 years, reprinting so many times that we estimated that 250,000 copies had been sold all over the world. Someone told me they had purchased a copy in Fiji!

If any painting has helped progress my career and put my name around, it was that single bull elephant with a black sky, standing in yellow grass. *Wise Old Elephant* became known with great affection as my 'Elephant in Boots'. Boots the Chemists was one of the main points of sale and must have done tremendously well out of my elephant. No doubt readers will think that I must have done well too – a royalty on each copy. It was not like that, I sold the copyright for £100 outright! However, the story has an amusing conclusion. In 1963, I was a guest for the third time on John Dunn's programme on Radio 2, with its Friday evening listenership of some 2,000,000 people. It is a live programme and we were talking about my 'Elephant in Boots': laughter all round. I said to John, 'If I go on plugging Boots like this, it's time they did something for me'; more laughter. Boots were obviously listening because, three days later, a gigantic box full of deodorants and hair sprays arrived for my wife, with 'the compliments of the company'. So my elephants have helped Avril, too.

March Sunlight

Going into print has its pitfalls. On the success of *Wise Old Elephant*, virtually every publisher in the United Kingdom rang me up and asked, 'Can we do an elephant? Name your price.' At that stage in my career, I had four daughters to educate and the blank cheques that I was being offered would help pay for their education. However, at the same time, I was getting the most appalling publicity in the mass media: 'Out goes that ghastly green woman (Tretchikoff), and now, so help me, you're buying elephants.' That warning signal appeared in the *News Chronicle*. I realised that the more people I had queuing up for my paintings and appreciating what I was doing for conservation, the greater the risk that I would become 'overpopular' and lose my credibility overnight. So I turned the offers down. I know that I made the right decision and at that time I moved into limited edition prints. However, my publishers asked me to do one more mass-produced print before taking this step and told me I could paint anything I liked. I chose an English landscape, *March Sunlight* and was almost in fear and dread of it becoming 'top of the pops'. I didn't want that – I had had enough of it. Both the publishers and I felt that there was little risk of this happening; it had no horses leaping out of breaking waves, no children crying, no green weeping Balinese girls, nor, indeed, any elephants! It was a plain statement of fact: a watery sun on an English winter's day. The print was duly published and, lo and behold, the trade judged it to be the top-selling print of 1967.

Inevitably, this success generated the usual rubbish written in the mass media. To my astonishment, on the 15 February of that year, in the diary column of the *London Evening Standard*, there was printed the most extraordinary piece of journalism that I have had the misfortune to read. The heading was 'Sex Symbols' and the article went on to state that 'the symbolism of *March Sunlight* is obvious to any amateur psychologist. The bursting buds on the elm trees represent awakening sex and the icy pools of water in the gateway represent sexual longing'. I could hardly believe it.

At the time, David Frost was doing a regular chat show on television and on one of these, he was talking about the mass market for prints. He had read this nonsense and invited me on the show. He read the piece to the audience who immediately collapsed into uncontrolled hysterics. The programme was running late and I only had a few minutes to explain this interpretation of my painting; all I could suggest was that the writer was either a sex maniac or a raving idiot!

I was paid £40 to go on the programme, and was given a car to take me to the studios from Waterloo Station and back. I knew now that this was the time to progress upwards into limited editions to retain my credibility. In the meantime, *March Sunlight* has been nicknamed, undeservedly, my 'sex painting' by those who know the absurd story.

RAILWAYS

RAILWAYS STARTED to join the planes in my life at about this time. Having inherited a passion for steam railways from my father, I now realised, as a professional artist, that the steam railway scene might offer the most magnificent material for paintings. Not then having the commitments and responsibilities that I acquired later in life, and being able to paint much more for myself, I seized every chance to put into practice the rigid training that Robin had given me.

Crewe, Swindon and York

I painted in the great engineering works at Crewe. At that time I believe they employed something like 6,000 men in the works and I am convinced that every one of them stopped work to look at what I was doing. Finally I was such a distraction that they had to put screens around me to enable a return to normal working.

My training the hard way with Robin Goodwin was now paying off; it takes some nerve to carry on undisturbed while 100 tons of locomotive is picked up and dangled overhead on a giant travelling crane. Coincidentally, the locomotive that featured in the painting called *Crewe Loco Works* was a British Rail standard 9F, 92011 which had never been 'out on the road'. It was brand new and little did I know that twelve short years later I would actually own one of her sister engines, 92203, which, at that time, had not even been built.

During those wonderful days of painting in Willesden sheds, Swindon Works and Crewe, I met, and have remained friends with ever since, some of the finest people I will ever know. In Swindon Works, one lovely old railway man used to bring freshly picked strawberries from his garden and put them on my easel every morning as he passed by to work.

I sold the painting of the paintshops at Swindon to British Railways for £60 and it was last seen hanging in their cafeteria in Swindon, covered in fish and chip grease – I wonder where it is now.

I mentioned earlier that the painting conditions at Heathrow were worse than in the streets of London. However, on reflection all these years later, I wonder how on earth I coped at all in some of the railway locations that I went to – even allowing for the fact that I was many years younger in those days. For example, on one occasion I painted a picture in York loco sheds, now the setting for the National Railway Museum. It was so cold that I had to be wrapped in three or four sweaters, and,

Hardly ideal conditions – Crewe Loco Works.

like in Willesden sheds, it always seemed to be snowing. Why on earth did I always choose midwinter? The snow was black by the time it hit the ground and the only thing that kept me going was encouragement from all the railway engine men who were watching, and who fortified me with endless cups of steaming hot tea from the nearest locomotive footplate.

All these places were, inevitably, 'filthy', but it was 'lovely' dirt and oil in the context of these marvellous sheds long since demolished. To add to all the litter and muck around me, I remember chucking my oily rags down into the inspection pit right next to me. Many years later, I went to the same place, now terribly clinical and cleaned up as the Railway Museum. The pits are now covered over: I wonder if my paint rags are still there?

King's Cross

Not only were the conditions cold and miserable, but often potentially dangerous as well. It seemed I always chose the worst places to sketch. I painted a picture called *Service by Night* which portrayed a night scene at King's Cross in the days of steam. Trains leave King's Cross Station and go straight into a tunnel; I chose to sketch by the tunnel mouth. Because of this, I had to be escorted out every day and have a railway man standing beside me while I worked. Being stupid, as I always was, I could easily have stepped over a rail and promptly got clobbered by an engine coming out of the tunnel behind me.

When the Eastern Region of British Railways purchased *Service by Night* for £60, which thrilled me, they said they would like to turn it into a poster, which excited me even more – I was going to have my work pasted up on station platforms all over the country! Inevitably, this meant that the painting had to be completely accurate in every possible detail, and I knew absolutely nothing about signalling, or anything else. When I finally completed it and showed it to the authorities, it was riddled with mistakes. I had a passenger train coming out of the picture on the lines on the right-hand side. That, I was told, was the milkyard. So it had to be painted out. Every signal light was wrong – how was I to know? Finally, after five or six attempts at getting it correct, it was passed by those who knew and went to

Waterlows, who printed railway posters. Several hundred copies were run off the machines. It was then that a major mistake was found that nobody had noticed, right in the foreground of the painting.

I had got the points wrong, which meant that the 'Flying Scotsman' would have derailed coming out of the platform. If the posters had been pasted up at the stations with this mistake, poor old British Railways would have been plagued by railway enthusiasts ringing them up every couple of minutes. An unfortunate employee of Waterlows had to alter every poster by hand with a pencil. I had thought this painting to be 'lost', after delivering it to British Rail in 1955. In fact, in the course of preparation for this book, I have discovered it to be part of the national collection in York Railway Museum.

Rolling Mills and Ships

A number of other exciting and interesting commissions were gradually beginning to come my way at this stage in my life. I was commissioned to paint a *Continuous Strip Rolling Mill* at the Steel Company of Wales works at Port Talbot, in South Wales. With the noise, and the heat, not to mention the sparks flying in all directions, it seemed like 'hell on earth'. The rolling mill itself, about the size of a three-storey house, was at one end of the factory which stretched for four hundred metres (¼ mile). In order to portray the vastness of this whole subject, I chose to perch myself with my easel, right up in the girders of the factory, near the roof. It was so hot that I stripped right down to my underclothes. Wearing boots and a safety helmet, but very little else, it was not a pretty sight!

I have always loved ships, but, being incurably romantic and living in the past, I would have no enthusiasm whatsoever to paint their modern counterparts. They look like travelling blocks of flats! However, in the 1960s when I was gradually getting a name, I met the management of the Blue Funnel Line in Liverpool and was asked to paint a couple of pictures of their lovely passenger and cargo ships, which sailed around the Far East. I remember meeting them in a pub in Liverpool and a deal was struck – if I were to give them the two paintings, in turn they would give Avril and myself a free trip on whichever ship of their fleet we chose, all around the Far East, to Japan and Indonesia. We took the opportunity to extend the visit to go right into Cambodia and many other places that I had only dreamed of visiting. We had to be paid a shilling a day to be 'members of the crew', but no one seemed to mind. It is rather nice to be able to create something that other people want and end up with a situation in which everybody is happy.

PORTRAITS

I N MY VIEW, there have been far too many art schools churning out far too many students for far too long. It is, surely, a sad reflection of the age in which we live to suggest that relatively few of those leaving college with ambition will actually achieve it, such is the competition. Perhaps it is the same with composing music, or acting; we are certainly often told that even those actors with names are 'resting'. Painters who are lucky enough to have achieved success in their own lifetime, and I am proud to be one of them, are often in public misconception supposed to have 'been dead 200 years'. Someone actually came up to me once and said, 'David, I thought you were dead.' If one does not actually suffer that particular indignity, then there are always the cases of mistaken identity.

For a number of years, there was a girl who worked in the BBC who believed I was the Bishop of Liverpool, my namesake. Try as I would, I could not convince her that to live in Godalming in Surrey, as I do, would be very inconvenient if I was the Bishop of Liverpool!

Being mistaken for another David Shepherd, I was once asked to umpire a cricket match. I have only played cricket twice in my life, once was at prep school in 1938, the other occasion was very many years later. By this time, I was deeply immersed in conservation, determined to raise money by whatever means, and I was invited to be 'non-playing' captain of the Lotus team, against the Parachute Regiment. It was a very exciting occasion, attended by a great crowd, at the Aldershot Officers' Club, and the whole event was jointly in aid of the Airborne Forces Museum and the David Shepherd Conservation Foundation. By 3:00 o'clock, we had all, inevitably, had far too much to drink and I was invited to play. In sheer terror, I 'padded-up', faced the bowling and hit the ball first time. I was so overwhelmed by my success that I swung my arms around in excitement and promptly knocked all the bails off. Despite this we raised a lot of money for two good causes on that afternoon.

I say all this because I am lucky to be known at all in my lifetime, but it is mainly for painting elephants. I do paint a number of other subjects, and portraits are some of my favourites. I have been incredibly lucky because I have only painted five or six portraits, and they have all been fairly important people, starting with Christ and you can't start higher than that! I have had the honour of painting Her Majesty Queen Elizabeth, the Queen Mother, Sheikh Zayed of Abu Dhabi, past President Dr Kaunda of Zambia and my wife, twice.

Avril

The first time I painted my wife, she had mumps. I suppose it was a bit cruel, but we were both busy, even in those days, and as she was lying in bed, it was the only chance that I had to paint her. So I hauled her out from her sick room, and made her sit. The portrait came off very well, bumps and all. This illustrates a point remembered from my lessons with Robin, that there is no better way than painting from life. Although portrait No1 of Avril, mumps and all, is in my attic and no one sees it, I consider it to be a better painting, though not very flattering to Avril, than the second one, painted many years later, which appears in this book. This latter portrait, through increased pressure of commitments at the time, could only be done from photographs.

The Reredos

I will be a lucky man indeed if I am remembered for anything I have painted after I am dead. (If I am, it will probably be *Wise Old Elephant*. 'Oh, he was the bloke who painted that elephant in Boots the Chemist.') The one picture that I would dearly love to be remembered by, among all others, is the painting of Christ that I did for the Army in 1964.

When I was asked if I might be interested in painting a 'reredos', for the Army Garrison Church at Bordon Camp, near Petersfield in Hampshire, I didn't even know what a reredos was. The Army chaplains were discussing the form that a memorial to commemorate all the regiments stationed at Bordon might take, when HM Treasury sanctioned the building of a new church. (As I write, more than thirty years later, it still hasn't been given the go-ahead.) All the usual ideas were put forward, but one chaplain, perhaps more enterprising than the others, suggested that I might be approached. I met them and accepted the invitation on the spot; I was so overwhelmed by the challenge to which I had committed myself that I

stopped my car in a lay-by on the way home and broke out into a cold sweat! (At that time the only portrait I had done was the one of my wife with mumps.)

The problems in undertaking such a challenge were enormous. First of all, I had to find a model, quite apart from the pose and the dress. Furthermore, I had an enormous amount of research to do because the great number of regiments that had been stationed at Bordon over the years all had to be represented in the form of cameos surrounding the central figure. On the point of pose and dress, the Army chaplains were super and very broadminded; they said, 'We don't want fat cherubs floating all over the place. We want a realistic portrayal of Christ as a man, which will bring the men into church.' The local paper in Farnham, where we were living at the time, found the model for me. They had heard of a chap who was working for the Forestry Commission nearby, who had come to be known as 'Jesus' by his 'mates' because he had grown his hair long. The journalist was so impressed with his appearance that he brought him up to my studio and the problem was solved.

Concerning the dress, I had remembered a film called *The Robe*. In this, Charlton Heston was dressed in a simple white costume tied around the waist with a cord, and with a lovely rust-red robe of homespun material over his shoulder. This is what I wanted; it seemed simple enough. I decided to go to the biggest theatrical costumiers in London as I thought they must be able to provide something. After all, even if you ask for 500 German soldiers for a film, they can fit you out. They told me that 'all the Christ costumes are out on hire'. This surprised me, because it was May, which is not a particularly religious month, surely. Instead they showed me Peter O'Toole's costume for Lawrence of Arabia – complete with bullet hole in the sleeve. I didn't want Peter O'Toole, I wanted Christ, and I walked out in a huff, but from that moment, everything seemed to fall into place in the most amazing way. Avril said, 'I'll make the thing.' We went up to London, walked straight into the first store in Oxford Street, and there was all the material we needed, in a sale, on the front counter.

I was so petrified at starting that five years went by. I finally got a phone call from the War Office. 'You have completed the painting, haven't you? We have engaged the Chaplain General to the Queen to consecrate it in a month's time.' I hadn't started it. I had 6 x 2.5 metres (20 x 8ft) of blank white canvas staring me in the face and I didn't even know if the model was still around; he was, he was still waiting and wondering what on earth was happening. I had visions of the Chaplain General consecrating half the painting and then coming back in a month's time to consecrate the rest! Nevertheless, in a blind panic, the whole painting was painted on time, although it was still wet when consecrated. The church was packed and the whole event was so emotional, my mother and I were crying our hearts out right the way through the service. That is the one painting that I want to be remembered by.

President Kaunda

Painting the former President of Zambia, Dr Kenneth Kaunda, also had its problems, although of rather a different sort. Because he was a busy man, I could only paint him when he was having a brief holiday in the Luangwa Valley National Park. With the heat and dust, and the ever-changing light, not to mention the hippos making revolting noises in the lagoon just behind me, this was hardly the ideal place to paint a Head of State. Nevertheless, with his great co-operation, we managed. There was no dais on which to put him so we piled a couple of tractor tyres on top of each other. We then put a Woolworths chair on top and sat him in that, under a tree. Being the good man he is, he was so helpful: I said, 'I don't like your shirt, Sir'; he said, 'OK, I'll borrow yours.'

In fact the conditions were so difficult that once again, I panicked. I just had to bash down whatever I could see in front of me and regard it simply as a working sketch which I would then take back to England. I would then work from that, together with photographs. Anglo American Corporation, who had commissioned the painting for their boardroom, naturally asked me how I got on, when we returned to Lusaka. I was so embarrassed that I refused to show them the result.

'I'm going back home and I am going to paint you a proper boardroom portrait.'

'No, that's not what we want. Let's see what you've done.'

They were really very nice about it. They insisted that they didn't want a 'boardroom' portrait.

'Let's see it.'

I finally showed it to them and they said, 'That's the best portrait we have ever seen of President Kaunda – we will have it as it is, blobs of paint and all.' It still hangs in their boardroom.

The painting I most want to be remembered by – but I expect I won't be!

Sheikh Zayed

It seems to me that Arabs have no sense of time. This was certainly proved when I accepted the commission and challenge to paint Sheikh Zayed of Abu Dhabi. After protracted arrangements through the Foreign Office and friends who live in the Gulf, I was told that I would be guaranteed five days when he would sit for me. I doubted this very much, but I packed up all my equipment and flew out to Abu Dhabi. I arrived at some unearthly hour in the morning, and the plane flew on to Bahrain, with all my equipment, easel, cloths, and toothbrush. I was stuck at 1:30 in the morning with only the clothes I stood up in. I rang the Trucial Oman Scouts, who had their camp in the town and for whom I had painted a picture some years previously. Mercifully, they were still up, having a Mess party, so they came out and rescued me. That problem was solved, at least, but now the real problems started. Although I had been 'promised' sittings over a guaranteed period, that apparently meant nothing, as I was soon to discover. No rudeness was intended, it just happens, and I should have realised that the Arabs have a different approach to life to mine. Days went by and time

and time again I was promised a guarantee of meeting the great man 'the next day'. So the next day my chums would drive me miles out into the desert to one of his many houses. When I arrived, there were always at least one hundred other Arabs waiting to meet him. Time meant nothing. You simply sat around in the desert and waited for something to happen. On the first three occasions, Sheikh Zayed didn't even see me: he got into his Mercedes and drove straight off over the sand into the distance; but after three weeks, by now a mental wreck, I was finally able to meet him, in the gardens in the middle of the town. He sat engaged in animated conversation with a friend of mine, in Arabic, and I realised that I would have to work from photographs. In a panic, I fired away with my camera and then returned to England.

When the film came back, only one of the thirty-six transparencies had come out; in the others I had cut off the top of his head! That is all I had to work from, but I did, and the portrait was extremely well received by all those concerned.

The Queen Mother

Painting the Queen Mother was like a breath of fresh air. I was commissioned to paint Her Majesty by the King's Regiment. I had obviously never painted royalty before, but I did know something of the problems. Innumerable establishments, civil and military, commission the appropriate royal portrait, so the easel on which the next painter in the queue is to paint the relevant member of the royal family is already set up in the household concerned. The staff of Clarence House could not possibly have been more friendly and I was accorded a wonderfully warm welcome. However, I was shown into a very dark room where I was to paint Her Majesty. I pointed out to her private secretary that it was not an ideal light; I wanted to see what I was doing! I was told that the previous portrait painter, much more famous than me, had painted Queen Elizabeth the Queen Mother in that very room – so perhaps I should consider doing the same. I had seen that particular painting, and I was just on the point of saying, slightly with tongue in cheek, 'so that is why the result was not that good', when the Queen Mother, almost unannounced, walked in.

I remember her saying something like, 'Is Mr Shepherd being difficult?'

'Yes,' came back the reply.

'Well, we had better find another room for Mr Shepherd to paint in, then.'

There followed a conducted tour around the ground floor of Clarence House and an alternative location was found for me straightaway. It was a lovely room overlooking the Mall, filled with sunshine and flowers.

Another potential problem concerned how I was to dress. I need not have worried. 'Oh, your painting clothes will be fine,' said her private secretary. He had not seen my painting clothes. I wonder if he expected me to wear a very expensive 'artist's outfit' – beret, pink sandals and all the rest of it, which I might have bought from Harrods. Not at all. My painting clothes consisted, and they still do, of a pair of trousers that I bought from a Sunday market for £8.50 many years ago. They are jolly good trousers. The point is that I wipe my brushes on the right leg while I am working. The result is that when I take the multi-coloured garment off in the evening after a hard day's work, the trousers stand up on their own. Nobody seemed to mind at Clarence House. When the Queen Mother came in for the first sitting, I remember her saying something like, 'what a fascinating collection of colours, Mr Shepherd'.

I was exceedingly lucky in the fact that I had more than my 'ration' of one-hour sittings – six, spread over five months. During all this time, we talked animatedly together and it is a wonder I did any work at all. Many subjects came up, from modern architecture and grandchildren, to drugs and Africa, and I felt very privileged indeed. Apart from anything else, it was such enormous fun and I have so many memories, many of which I would never put into print; the Queen Mother has very strong ideas about certain aspects of modern life, and she is very trusting. Her informality put me at ease at once. She kept me waiting twenty minutes on one occasion. Who was I to complain? She came into the room and said, 'Mr Shepherd, I am so sorry to be late. I have been up the road having coffee with my daughter.' One other moment that I cherish is when I was invited to have luncheon after the last sitting. I felt that I should dress rather more appropriately so I put a suit on – always a great effort for me.

When she came into the room the Queen Mother said, 'You are looking very smart today, Mr Shepherd.'

'Yes, Ma'am, I know. I am having lunch with you.'

'Your painting clothes would have been perfectly all right. It's quite informal. It's only you and the Duchess of Gloucester.'

Happy memories indeed.

STEAM ENGINES

IT WAS IN 1967 that the success of my 'Jumbo' paintings was to play a rather unexpected part in my story. I have already described how, after completing my training with Robin in 1953, I was able to indulge myself and, because of the few commitments I had at the time, I was able to paint railway subjects (I even managed to sell a couple of these for £60 each and they are now part of the national collection in York Railway Museum). However, getting married and taking on family commitments meant that I had to earn a living and painting railway subjects just for the fun of it was pushed into the background. In any case, at that time, steam trains were all around us; perhaps it is human nature only to notice something when it has gone. Then, in 1967, things did start to happen, and fast. It was dawning on the railway enthusiasts in Britain that our steam age was dying. Hundreds of our beloved locomotives were being towed away for scrap every month, and they decided that something had to be done about it.

By this time, I had been painting wildlife for a number of years and the increasing success that this was bringing me resulted in a very considerable backlog of private commissions which kept me in my studio seven days a week 'painting elephants'. However, the magic 'pull' of Guildford loco sheds, right on my doorstep, and the great steam shed of Nine Elms near Waterloo, both then in their death throes, finally became irresistible. I found myself dashing along to Guildford at every available moment in the evenings to record on canvas, in a last feverish rush, something of the fast-vanishing steam era.

Black Prince and *The Green Knight*

It was at Guildford and Nine Elms that I got the preservation bug. I was meeting enthusiasts who, like myself, were desperate to try to save something of our steam age.

I began to dream of owning my very own steam locomotive. Now, so many years afterwards, the very thought makes my hair stand on end!

In 1967 I had a major one-man exhibition of wildlife paintings in New York which sold out on the first evening. In a state of euphoria, and acting on impulse, I picked up the telephone and spoke to a senior friend of mine in British Railways.

'I want to buy two steam engines, Bob.'

'Why on earth do you want two?'

'Because two are more exciting than one!'

I must have sounded completely mad to British Rail, but then there were plenty of lunatics around like me at that time. We were buying engines as though they were packets of cornflakes. British Rail deserves the greatest credit for taking us seriously. 'You're in luck, David, we have just overhauled 92203; she's probably the best Standard 9 we've got so you can have her.' So, as a result

Black Prince *and* Green Knight *on the East Somerset Railway.*

of that telephone call, I found myself the proud but totally bewildered and slightly frightened owner of two enormous steam locomotives. Number 75029, built in 1954, had cost me £2,200; number 92203, only eight years old, brand new, cost just £3,000. Both locomotives were in full working order, and together they weighed over 200 tons! Neither had ever been near a scrapyard.

Several months later I went up to Crewe South locomotive shed in Cheshire, where my two locomotives had been 'dumped' for my collection, and panicked. I had no money left, no home for them and an eviction order to get rid of them. Locomotives weighing over 100 tons in full working order are very heavy indeed and not that easy to take away!

It was through one of those funny twists of fate that a first home for my locomotives was found. The Army operated the Longmoor Military Railway in Hampshire near Bordon, and it was for Bordon Garrison Church that I had painted my picture of Christ, mentioned earlier. It was during the research for that painting that I had met

an army officer who happened to be stationed at Bordon and who was also a railway enthusiast. It was through him, quite unofficially, that the locomotives I had bought had a home to go to.

After long and protracted negotiations lasting eleven months with the bureaucratic side of British Railways, who were not in the least interested in my steaming my two locomotives in mint condition down their railway lines (which seemed the most logical way to get them to their destination), I finally won the battle. The two engines steamed from Crewe down through the Midlands to Longmoor on the weekend of Saturday and Sunday 7 and 8 April, 1968.

It was a momentous occasion. Many thousands of people lined the route, and on the engines' arrival at the Longmoor Military Railway in Hampshire, I was completely drained with the emotion of it all; a lot of people thought I was mad as I went around patting *Black Prince.* That is what steam engines do to me!

In retrospect, it is amazing what we achieved at the Longmoor Military Railway during our all-too-brief stay there. It proved once again that it is not *what* you know

but *who* you know. Through the good offices of our friendly colonel (and a general higher up in the military echelon), various other mainline steam engines that had been bought by lunatics like me came to join the collection, laying the foundations of what could have been a magnificent steam centre. We ended up with a collection of some six railway coaches, half a dozen wagons, and six mainline steam locomotives, and the War Office, I suspect, never found out! We knew the Longmoor Military Railway was finally going to die, and we were determined to save it. However, the scheme was finally 'killed off' by half a dozen malicious people who were determined at any length to make sure that David Shepherd and his 'mad friends' would never be allowed to ruin the Hampshire countryside with all the noise and dirt and smoke – 'we will never be able to play tennis in our gardens again'. (The Military Railway had been there since after World War I.)

The campaign against me personally was vicious to the extreme, as I put up with verbal abuse as well as a torrent of nasty letters about me in the local press. Steam engines not only bring out the best in people; they certainly bring out the worst! We had to get out – but that is another story.

The East Somerset Railway

The long struggle to find a permanent home for our steam engines then started. A number of my friends had joined me from the very early days and we looked at no less than thirty-one different places before we found a little village in Somerset called Cranmore. We did not start with very much. We had a derelict station and signal box and two acres of land covered in stinging nettles and old corrugated iron. Since those days in the early 1970s we have built a magnificent Victorian steam locomotive shed and workshop; we now own three miles of track, have fully restored the station and are a registered charity. The whole of this operational steam railway, which is open to the public every day in the summer and on weekends, runs a regular steam-hauled passenger train service, operated by a dedicated and enthusiastic team of volunteers and undoubtedly gives pleasure to many thousands.

The two halves of my life, the preservation of steam locomotives and the conservation of wildlife, came together on 20 June 1975. On that day, my friend Prince Bernhard of the Netherlands, then the International President of the World Wildlife Fund, came over from Holland to open the railway officially, and all in aid of the World Wildlife Fund. We raised some £7,000 on that

My new toy!

afternoon and afterwards a friend of mine wrote to me: 'How very appropriate to have such fun running up and down with your two steam engines, to help save elephants.'

I am proud and thrilled that I have been able to set this enterprise up. If it had not been for the success of my elephant paintings I would not have been able to buy *Black Prince* and *The Green Knight* in the first place – no wonder I am crazy about jumbos.

The Zambezi Sawmills Railway

I suppose it was inevitable that eventually my passion for preserving steam locomotives would spread to Africa but I never dreamed of the extent to which this would happen. It was in 1971 that I took on a World Wildlife Fund project to buy a Bell Jet Ranger helicopter to present to Zambia to combat poaching. I took seven of my paintings out to Reno in Nevada and, together with other paintings and items donated by generous people and

organisations, we raised the money in twenty minutes. A few months later I flew out to Zambia with the helicopter and presented it to President Kaunda.

It just happened that at this time the Zambezi Sawmills Railway was closing down.

I had first become acquainted with this extraordinary old railway on my first visit to Zambia in 1964. I had been driving away from the Victoria Falls and back to Livingstone when I noticed a railway track crossing the road at right-angles and disappearing into the distance. Running alongside the line which, to put it mildly, looked as though someone had dropped it from a great height, was a dirt road. I drove up it. I soon came to a group of ancient and dusty wooden buildings, one of which was obviously a locomotive shed, built of massive timber supports and beams and with a tin roof. Behind it stood a tall and shady palm tree. A beautiful jacaranda tree was in full flower just behind the wreck of an ancient steam engine standing upon piles of wooden blocks with all its wheels missing. A corrugated-iron water tower was covered in bougainvillaea, looking glorious in full flower. Inside the two-road shed there was even an inspection

pit, although it was now full of water and frogs.

Locomotive bogies, wheels and axles were everywhere, all disappearing gradually in the long, dusty, golden grass of an African dry season. The sun caught the maze of cobwebs which were enveloping these various pieces of railway equipment, strewn in total disorder wherever I looked. Other cannibalised engines in various states of decay were lying around, some leaning over at precarious angles and looking as though they would topple at any moment. They were resting on a track that had long since disappeared into the vegetation and sand. Some had sizeable trees growing through their cabs or through the gaping cavities where the driving wheels once turned. The searing hot sun of many African summers had burned the sides of the tenders and, under the peeling and faded paintwork, the lettering of past owners was revealed.

I kept a watchful eye out for snakes. I had been told that the old locomotives and coaches provided a cool and shady resting place for many a cobra wanting to escape the hot African sun. Honey bees were nesting in one of the holes of a locomotive boiler from which the plugs had long since disappeared. I fought my way through the undergrowth and climbed up on the cab of one of the ancient engines. Here was the greatest surprise of all. The engine was complete, with all the gauges and fittings. Most of the locomotives still sported their whistles and, on their buffer beams, the heavy and beautiful solid cast-brass number plates. Obviously these items didn't have the intrinsic value that they had in England – back home, everything would have been stolen months before.

Being an inveterate collector of such items, I went back to the main offices of the company, another collection of dusty wooden buildings. I asked the general manager whether it might be possible to have some of the number plates off the 'old engines in the scrap line'. His answer amazed me: 'Yes, I'll get someone to take some of them off for you but I would like to point out that the engines are not on the scrap line. When we get around to it, we will tow them up to Mulobezi and give them an overhaul.' Then, with an absolutely straight face, he went on to say: 'But you know, the problem is, it's awfully difficult to get the spare parts.' Considering the locomotives dated from 1896, I wasn't the least surprised!

The Zambezi Sawmills Railway seemed to belong to another century, and perhaps the most remarkable part of it was the use of a motley collection of ancient road vehicles which used to run on the railway system – it simply meant that they had had the road wheels taken off and railway wheels put on and were thus adapted, in a highly precarious fashion, to run on the rails.

With the imminent closing down of logging operations in the forest in 1971, the BBC and I made a documentary for television, *Last Train to Mulobezi*.

To record the complete story of the railway, it was essential to have one of the cars in the film. Unfortunately, the whole fleet had long since expired and been dumped in the bush. However, we did manage to find a 1938 Ford Prefect, which we got going for just long enough to feature in the film before she too finally died. The logging operations closed down at Mulobezi after we completed the film and I realised with foreboding that most of the ancient locomotives and coaches, some dating from the last century, would be dumped forever in the scrap line, to rot gently in the African sunshine. It was too much to bear; once again, without a thought for the future, I asked President Kaunda if I could have one. He gave me two: No 993, a Class 7 built in Glasgow in 1896, and still in full working order; and the 'Queen of Mulobezi', their mainline Class 10 built in Glasgow in 1922. Not only was I now the owner of two engines, but they had also given me a beautiful 1927 vintage sleeping car, and it was still complete with its magnificent mahogany panelling and green leather bunks.

It seems I will never learn! I was now heaping upon my shoulders even more railway problems. I was the proud owner of two large steam locomotives and a coach, in the heart of a landlocked African country. How on earth could I ever get them home? We started investigating the possibility of going over the bridge into Rhodesia – still a white colony. This was a time of political instability and the famous Victoria Falls Bridge, which spans the Zambezi river and forms the border between Zambia and Rhodesia, was closed. Logically, therefore, this meant that I should look to going northwards to Mombasa through 'black Africa'. However, after talking to a number of friends in Zambia, they all pointed out that this would be a complete waste of time. So, more for amusement than anything else (this is where the story takes on a flavour of complete fantasy), I thought that I would just go along and have a little talk with the customs officials on the Zambian side of the railway bridge over the river. Thinking I should come straight to the point I said, 'I have two steam engines and a coach. Can I take them over the bridge into Rhodesia?' To my amazement, and with an absolutely straight face, he replied, 'Yes. There is no problem, you can call them your own "personal effects"' – all 200 tons of them!

I have never discovered whether the official was trying to be funny, or being serious. I did know, however, that it was not going to be as simple as that. There was only one man who could solve the problem and that would be President Kaunda. I was invited out to talk to him when

An engine comes home after 78 years.

he was taking a brief and well earned holiday in his favourite Luangwa Valley. He at once gave his personal blessing to my request; this took the form of a state document, for 'immediate action from the Office of the President'. I wonder how many other Heads of State would have bothered with this? President Kaunda was different. He did bother about these sorts of things.

It is amazing what one can achieve when armed with such a document. In almost no time at all, the locomotives and coach made their historic journey over the bridge, in the middle of sanctions, and down to Bulawayo. There, sadly, the Class 10, the mainline engine, had

reluctantly to be stored because my sponsor, who was financing the whole exercise, was not prepared to pay for the two locomotives and the coach to come back to the United Kingdom. The Class 7 and coach journeyed down through Mozambique to Beira for shipment back to England. They reached Manchester docks and, causing total traffic chaos, journeyed down the M1 motorway. They have a home at the East Somerset Railway where they add to the immense tourist attraction that this enterprise now is.

THE ARMED FORCES

I HAVE THE SERVICES to thank for a large part of my success as an artist, and for the exciting times that I have had with them. In particular, I have enjoyed a very special relationship with the Royal Air Force. Although I have never actually worn a uniform of any sort in my life, I have flown in no fewer than 32 different types of aircraft and most of them were military.

The Royal Air Force

Between 1965 and 1969 No 3 Group, Royal Air Force Bomber Command asked me to do several paintings for them and this meant flying in V Bombers which, at that time, were our main nuclear deterrent. One of the greatest challenges was to paint a night-flight refuelling exercise for 90 Squadron, of which I am proud to be an honorary member. This meant flying in the first of the three V Bombers, the Vickers Valiant. At my advanced age even then, it was a wonder I survived. I had to pass the very strict medical examination to see if I was fit enough. This included going through a decompression test; the theory being, presumably, that it is cheaper to kill you in a decompression chamber than in the actual aeroplane. The idea was to take me up to an assimilated height of 9,150 metres (30,000ft), as if in the aeroplane. Then, a chap working a lot of dials outside the chamber would create the effects of an immediate emergency or malfunction, such as a window blowing out of the aircraft. I would then be descended at speed right down to ground level!

They shut the door and I sat in my flying suit opposite a Royal Air Force officer going through the same treatment. He had obviously done it before because he was calmly reading *Country Life*, while I was shaking at the knees. Everything was fine until the chap outside pulled the switch to 'blow the window out'. The pressure on my head immediately became so great that I thought my skull was going to crack. I was sure I would be dead within seconds. I was connected by a lead to the operator outside the chamber and I was yelling to him to stop, and send me up again. However, nobody seemed to realise that there was a malfunction and my lead was not working. It was by sheer chance that the officer opposite happened to look up and, noticing my impending doom, told them to send me up again. With apologies all round,

the operator said, 'If you can survive that, you can survive anything. You're OK.'

I now had to go through the pre-flight briefing. For what seemed like several minutes, after being stripped down to my underclothing, a Royal Air Force chap proceeded to pile just about everything conceivable on to my suffering body: my flying suit, my parachute, a bone dome, an oxygen mask, and lots of other things which I thought it was probably best to ignore as I would not have understood them anyway. As he was dressing me, he was telling me what I should do if I had to bale out at 9,150 metres (30,000ft). He was talking so fast that, again, it was all quite beyond me. But I had infinite faith in the Royal Air Force. In any case, after piling all these things on me, the chap said, 'You'll freeze to death anyway.' To anyone, like myself, who had never gone through this sort of experience, and who was inevitably somewhat tensed up, this 'good old British sense of humour' was actually the very best way to put me at my ease; I knew I was in the hands of professionals who would take good care of me.

We took off for the five-hour sortie in the late afternoon and, as the setting sun created the most magical scene, I filmed the Valiant flying alongside us, and its vapour trail; both were bathed in a pink light. That little piece of movie must now be quite historic.

The conditions in a Valiant were very cramped for an extra seat. I had to sit on a sling attached between the seats of the co-pilot and the pilot. After a couple of hours, the strain began to tell. Apart from all the equipment that I had heaped on me, I had my movie camera for the early part of the flight, plus my sketch-book equipment and a torch. By now in the pitch dark, we nudged up ever closer to the Valiant above us until we were only twelve metres (40ft) below the tail of the tanker. Both of us were flying at approximately 400 knots. The whole of the underneath of the tanker aircraft was floodlit and as the drogue floated towards us in the dark to attach itself to our probe, the pilot's hands were on the throttle to ensure that we were flying at precisely the same speed as it. We made perfect contact the first time, as I expected. Towards the end of the flight I began to feel very queasy indeed and only just avoided disgracing myself before we landed.

A painting such as this creates enormous problems.

The Royal Air Force will only accept the painting if it is technically correct – every detail has to be right. The problem is even greater when one is confronted with the complete cockpit of a nuclear bomber. All the needles on the instruments had to be exactly where they should be and I hadn't a clue what it all meant. For the best part of a morning, I had to sit with the pilot in an aircraft on the ground looking at every dial, to ensure that I got all the details of every instrument correct as if actually flying. Not only did I have to incorporate all this into the painting, but also, looking through the windscreen, I had to portray the tanker lit up in the dark above us.

Shortly after this, I had a number of flights in the last of the V Bomber trio, the Handley Page Victor.

Some years later, by which time I was doing fewer paintings for the Services, it became apparent that the most exciting and glamorous, to many, of the V Bomber trio, the much-loved delta wing Vulcan, was coming to the end of its twenty-five-year service life. I was all the more determined, therefore, to be one of the very few civilians who have flown in all three V Bombers. There was no likelihood of a commission actually to paint one, but I decided to telephone a friend in 35 Squadron at Scampton, anyway, to try my luck. I was not sure of the response. Should I have gone through the official channels? I suspect that if I had, I might well still be waiting and the reply could well have been negative. Once again, the informal approach worked. 'Of course, David, I am sure we can arrange something – come up and see us next week when we are going on a seven-hour training sortie.'

Once again, after the statutory pre-flight briefing, we all piled into our Vulcan and off we went. An extra crew member in a Vulcan has to sit sideways, several feet below the pilot and co-pilot, facing the opposite wall. Within minutes I was feeling sick, and within half an hour I was beginning to disgrace myself. I was utterly miserable. Suicide was the first thought. I asked rather sheepishly if we could go home. No, I had to 'sit it out'. The flight was seven hours, and that was that.

We were scheduled to fly over the Isle of Skye. A great friend of ours who is a retired admiral lives in a croft on this lovely island and I had rung up the previous evening to tell him to look out for a Vulcan flying over his roof. I would be in it! I told the crew this before we took off and they decided to give our friend a 'show'. As we were approaching the island, the pilot and co-pilot beckoned me to climb the ladder and have a look. I was now beginning to feel like death; however, with a supreme effort, I climbed up to see what was happening. I will never forget the sight. It seemed that we were going to whip the tops of the waves as we zoomed up into the island between the mountains. Then, just as I was about to collapse rapidly down the ladder again, we flew over a ridge and down over Roddy's chimney. I'm sure he got the shock of his life.

When we landed back at Scampton, I was feeling more dead than alive. However, I recovered very quickly and I was my old self within half an hour. The flight crew were super. 'If we had told you what it was going to be like, David, you might never have come with us.' I was told that a lot of extra passengers in Vulcans are often air-sick. They told me that I was the cleanest and best behaved passenger that they had ever had.

Another happy experience with the Royal Air Force brought conservation into the picture as well. I was in Germany as a guest of the RAF police, raising money for wildlife conservation, and I gave a couple of my 'talk shows' to Royal Air Force audiences. Collectively the evenings raised £7,000 and at the end of the second show, a guest in the front row of the audience came up to me and said, 'Jolly marvellous raising all that money to help save elephants, David. Would you like a flight in one of my Harrier Jump Jets tomorrow?' My response was prompt and positive. I had done my homework and knew that he was the Commanding Officer of No 1 Fighter Squadron from RAF Wittering, on a visit to Germany.

It was arranged the next day. I was passed as fit by the medical officer who simply tapped me with his stethoscope and said, 'You're OK'. That pleased me no end because I am quite convinced that I am the most geriatric person ever to have flown in a Harrier. The following morning, I flew around the skies of western Germany for a couple of hours – I should point out that it was a two-seater aircraft! Particularly memorable was the moment, just as we were coming in to land, when my pilot said, 'Shall we stop, go backwards and do that again?'; truly a remarkable aircraft, and an amazing feeling. The Royal Air Force have certainly been very good friends to me, and it was so appropriate that my painting, *Winter of '43 Somewhere in England* (in this book), raised a worthwhile sum for the Royal Air Force Benevolent Fund as a small token of thanks.

The Army

Many commissions have come my way over the years from the Army, and I have made many friends in the Army Air Corps, the Parachute Regiment and the SAS. Between them, they have commissioned more than twenty paintings from me, covering all aspects of their operations from World War II, the Malayan Emergency, and the Gulf War. Every commission presented its own problems, particularly as, as always, due to my training, I believe that the best way is the hard way: go to the actual location, relive the subject as near as you can, and the result will be all that much better. This has also resulted in my flying in helicopters and driving tanks in many different parts of the world – all very exciting and fun.

The Army Air Corps own some twelve pictures of mine, painted over many years. The first I did for them cost them £28! In return they have flown me all around Malaya in their little Auster 9s, long since gone. On one particular occasion, we were flying below the jungle tree tops, ascertaining whether it might be safe to 'have a go' and land on an obviously long-deserted and neglected airstrip, which had almost disappeared under long grass. Once again, it was no foolhardy gesture; the professionalism of the pilot ensured that I would survive and we landed safely.

I was asked to paint the Rhine crossing in World War II, for the Parachute Regiment. A major problem arose right from the start and it once again proved that it helps to know people in 'high places'. This time it was General Sir John Hackett, 'Shan' Hackett to his friends, who was commanding the British Army of the Rhine. He had said to me on a previous occasion, when I was painting the Battle of Arnhem, that if I ever needed any help, just to let him know.

I was well briefed on the Rhine crossing and the Army wanted to show me, at the correct time of day, the exact line of flight of the aircraft involved in the operation. This obviously meant flying over the Rhine itself. The Army Air Corps provided a Beaver, a small transport plane, carrying just a few passengers. I had flown in one of these aircraft many times and everything was fine until they told me, just before take off from Manston in Kent, that it was almost 'out of hours' before a major overhaul. It only had a couple of hours flying time remaining and we used both of those hours up, I cannot really remember why. Whatever the reason, we were stuck at Royal Air Force Station Wildenwrath with a 'dead' Beaver. We could not go any further. Something had to be done. I decided to play the final trump card in the pack and ring Shan. I actually managed to get through to him personally and, as friendly as ever on the other end of the telephone, he said, 'Don't worry, David, just sit tight.' An hour or so later, a new Beaver arrived especially for me. A colonel had come with me to help me on the exercise and, as we walked out to the aircraft, I could not help feeling rather proud of myself. My colonel friend said, 'I am a colonel. You're not even in the bloody Army – I couldn't do that!'

My painting *Arnhem Bridge, The Second Day* has to be one of the most emotive paintings I have ever been asked to do. A subject such as this inevitably involves an enormous amount of research and to convey the atmosphere of such a moment in our military history, I was determined to get every detail right. To achieve this, I made two private visits to Arnhem with officers who took part in the operation. Furthermore, I was a guest on some of the annual Arnhem pilgrimages, when, to help the painting further, I met and made friends with many brave Dutch civilians in the town.

The town of Arnhem must, as much as any of the other famous scenes of battle of World War II, evoke many emotional memories for those who took part. Having a very strong sense of recent history as I do, through my interest in World War II as a child and my art training which perhaps gave me that extra perception of things around me, I could almost 'feel' the houses, the bullet-scarred trees and the shell-scarred bridge talking to me.

General 'Johnny' Frost insisted on almost hanging his head over my shoulder all the time I was painting the picture. After all, he led the battalion on the bridge and he remembered the operation as vividly as though it had happened the day before. I had to get every possible detail correct to satisfy him. 'No, you can't put that burnt-out truck there. It was just over there' – I had to move it three inches to the left on the canvas! I believe the only thing I was really allowed to put where I wanted was the smoke.

I obviously succeeded in portraying something of the feeling of that historic battle because I was paid a great compliment by Cornelius Ryan after he had written *A Bridge too Far*. He signed a copy of the book for me just before he died. Shan Hackett himself, who dropped in with the 4th Brigade, said, 'David, I reckon you know more about Arnhem than anybody else does now'; a compliment indeed from a very brave man.

The second painting of Arnhem that I was asked to do was of 'the Cauldron'. This was the name given to the bloody battle that took place around the Hartestein Hotel and the crossroads in the village of Oosterbeck, just a few miles from Arnhem. During the later stages of the battle, the British and Germans were shooting at each other through the dressing stations on the crossroads and all hell was let loose. Flying a white flag, a German 'half track' came up the road and the senior German officer met Shan Hackett. It was agreed that there would be an interval of twenty minutes during which the wounded would be taken out to safety. Then the fighting could restart. My painting was to record this rare moment of chivalry in modern warfare.

My research proved not only fruitful, but fascinating. Two corners of the crossroads had been completely rebuilt since the war, and as I tried to discover what they actually looked like at the time, I was passed from one Dutch civilian to another until finally I met a lady who quite casually announced that she thought she had some old photographs up in the attic. Apparently, these had been taken by her late husband who had actually walked out with his camera right in the middle of the bloody fighting. The photographs gave me exactly what I wanted. The Hartestein Hotel is now a museum to commemorate the battle and my painting hangs there.

Painting for the Army has certainly had its lighter moments. I was commissioned by the Somerset and Cornwall Light Infantry to paint a commemorative picture of the presentation of Colours to the regiment in Gibraltar, by Lord Harding. In an ideal world, the artist should have the opportunity to go to a dress rehearsal of such an event so that he can choose the spot from which to paint the picture and sort out all other such details. This was not to be so for me; I could only spare the time to go on the night before the actual day of the event and had little idea of what to expect.

I was told that I would be given special permission to walk out into the middle of the parade at a given signal, quickly take my photographs and then immediately return to the audience. To get at least a vague idea of the point from which I would take my pictures, I had to ask all those important people present to stand with me on the parade ground the previous evening. We then marked the chosen spot on the parade ground with whitewash.

The day of the great event dawned, and what a dawn it was! Instead of a glorious blue Mediterranean sky, it was pouring with rain. We took our places in the audience. The band commenced marching backwards and forwards across the parade ground before the ceremony. I watched in horror as my whitewashed spot rapidly disappeared under hundreds of marching feet. All I could do was run out from the audience at the appropriate moment, hoping that I could remember where the spot had been. I did, but all the important people were several feet out of position. Instead of seeing Lord Harding presenting the Colours, which I should have done, all I could see, so it seemed at the time anyway, was my vision blotted out by the back view of a rather large Army chaplain! In a complete panic, I fired away with the camera in every possible direction and ran back to the audience.

Returning home to England, I sent the film off to be processed. Back it came. There was nothing on it, it was completely blank. In a crisis such as this, one cannot really expect the regiment and all the VIPs to go all the way back to Gibraltar to do it all again. However, fate always seems to come to my rescue. In desperation, it was arranged that I would go to the regimental depot at Shrewsbury where they had found a lance-corporal who was about the same size as Lord Harding, peeling spuds in the cookhouse. We tied an army blanket to a broomstick and persuaded him to kneel down on a cushion and 'present the Colours' to another lance-corporal who was equally obliging. I did the whole painting from the invaluable help provided by those two gentlemen and I am sure it was their finest hour in the regiment!

Considering the appalling problems, the completed painting was actually very well received by the Somerset and Cornwall Light Infantry, but I was soon faced with another dilemma. After several months, by which time the painting had been hung in the Officers' Mess and been seen by all those involved, discussions had apparently taken place as to whether they wanted complete historical accuracy, or just a little 'artist's licence'. Because it was a windy day and pouring with rain, the men, all lined up in No 1 dress, had their chin straps down to stop their hats blowing off into the Mediterranean; historical accuracy. However, it seemed that with the passage of time the demand for artist's licence won the day: they wanted the chin straps up over the peak of the cap because it looked smarter. I had to paint all the chin straps out, and with oil painting, this created a potential problem. As I knew from previous experience, when a dark patch is overpainted lighter, the dark paint underneath can begin to show through. I have a ghastly feeling that now, with the dark painting coming through on the chins of the men, it is highly possible that they all look as though they need a shave!

Many other paintings I have done for the military evoke so many memories for me, but there is no space here to recall them all. A brief journey with the SAS very many years ago from Tobruk in Libya, down on to the edge of the Sahara Desert, gave me some wonderful material for my painting of the Long Range Desert Group, in their clandestine operations in North Africa behind the German lines. I was commissioned to paint the Gulf War and as I was unable to go to the scene of battle myself, I had to work from photographs. We had great fun working together for my research, and at one time it seemed that I was having Lynx or Gazelle helicopters from Hampshire landing in my garden almost every week. The Army Air Corps obviously wanted to show me the photographs from which to work, and it was pointed out to me that it was not only quicker but much more convenient to come over in a Lynx than drive over in a Ford Escort – after all, it was all 'pilot training'.

I was also invited by the 'Green Howards' to paint two pictures depicting their very stressful time in Northern Ireland when a number of their soldiers were lost at the hands of the IRA. I feared that I would be asked to paint what could be called a 'blood and guts painting', but happily, this is not what they wanted. They wanted a painting portraying the utter boredom of their soldiers going out on foot patrol into the dingy and graffiti-ridden streets of Belfast republican areas such as the Ardoyne. I made several visits to Northern Ireland to do my research and one took me down to Forkill. This small place, in the heart of so-called 'bandit country', was nevertheless set in the midst of green, rolling hills, and it seemed utterly peaceful at the time of my visit. In fact, a large number of the villagers were, no doubt, openly supporting the IRA.

However, the Ardoyne really brought home to me what the British Army has experienced for so long during 'the troubles'. I wanted to see for myself, so I walked into this most sinister of places with a foot patrol. Wherever I looked, the walls were covered with malicious anti-British graffiti, most of the words of which are quite unrepeatable. This is what the soldiers had to put up with and I felt for them. I experienced at first hand something of that when I was physically spat at by a group of women, most of whom were pregnant. Because I was backed up by the Parachute Regiment, they had immediately assumed that I was Special Branch; hence the welcome. However, this treatment from those who were to be depicted in the painting did actually help. When the painting was unveiled, the colonel of the regiment immediately said, 'You can almost smell it.'

Painting a picture for the SAS of the siege of the Iranian Embassy in London certainly had its moments, too. It seemed that half the country had watched the live television shots of the siege from outside the building, but the regiment wanted me to depict what had actually gone on inside. I obviously had to see for myself, but my request to enter was immediately turned down by the Metropolitan Police. 'It's a very sensitive area, no one is allowed inside.' We endeavoured, therefore, to recreate the action in a building with a similar staircase, but this did not work and turned out to be hilarious. This particular building was actually an antique shop, if one could call it that; it was filled with treasures, priced at £20,000 and upwards. There was even a beautiful Van Dyke portrait hanging on the wall up the stairs. The owners of the establishment seemed to enjoy the whole scenario as much as we all did. They did not seem in the least perturbed at the prospect of SAS soldiers in their full gas equipment with weapons pushing people down the stairs, past the Van Dyke and through and around all the priceless pieces of antique furniture. Miraculously, nothing was damaged.

Sadly, despite all this wonderful co-operation from all concerned, it did not work. We decided to have another go at the Metropolitan Police and, this time, my request was granted, but with reservations. I was told to meet the chief inspector at exactly 11 o'clock on Tuesday, and I would be escorted around the back of the building. In retrospect, I cannot really understand the reason for all this tight security – anyone could have walked in through the back of the building as all the windows had gone.

I met the aforesaid gentleman at the appropriate time and, as we were walking around the front of the building, some dozen or more chaps appeared from around corners, all carrying heavy holdalls and looking, very unsuccessfully, like gas board workers. As they descended on us, I realised who they were. It was the SAS who had come all the way up from their depot because they were determined to show me exactly what had happened at the height of the operation. One Metropolitan Police officer on his own realised that he could do very little about the situation and he was awfully nice about it. 'OK, boys, come on in.' We all piled in through the back of the building. Once inside, off came the caps, the holdalls were opened, and on went the gas equipment, masks, and all the paraphernalia appropriate for the operation. For the next two hours, all the high tension of the operation was re-enacted especially for me, including the smoke.

The moment I had to portray in the painting was when the hostages were all being pushed down the stairs at the end of the operation to get them out of the building. One of the apparent hostages actually turned out to be a terrorist who pulled out a grenade and he was shot on the stairs. Outside, while all this was going on, the hustle and bustle of London carried on normally – no one had any idea of what was going on just a few yards away inside No 11 Prince's Gate!

Meanwhile the chief inspector who had allowed us in was standing, with his arms folded, with an expression of total resignation on his face. 'I want a bloody print of this bloody painting when you have done it.' We gave him a copy with great pleasure.

Project Tiger

Because I get excited about most big things and therefore have an enthusiasm to paint quite a considerable variety of different subjects, there is a link between tigers,

Lancaster Bombers and HMS *Ark Royal*.

By 1971, the tiger was on the brink of extinction with only 1,800 left in India. Because of this desperate situation, the World Wildlife Fund launched Project Tiger. As I owed so much to wildlife, even in those days, I decided to play my part and paint my very first tiger picture. I had never experienced the thrill of seeing a tiger in the wild so I journeyed all the way to India, but with so many poisoned or shot, I failed to see one.

I came back to England and went down to John Aspinall's Howlett's Zoological Park in Kent. John has a large collection of tigers and they are all 'his friends'; much has been said and written about the fact that he goes in and plays with eight Bengal tigers at a time and comes away unscathed. I have seen him do it. When I arrived, he said, 'You can go in with Zarif. He is quite friendly.' I had never met a tiger before, tame or otherwise, without something in between me and it, but on John's assurance that I would be alright, I went through the big gateway in the fencing which clanged shut behind me. This woke the tiger up and he came pounding towards me like a steam locomotive. I just stood there, my heart thumping like another steam locomotive. I looked round and to my astonishment, John was still outside the enclosure! He said, just in time, 'Just stand still while he gets to know you.' I had no idea what that really meant. Zarif arrived, I could have jumped on his back; he was huge. First of all, he rubbed his head up and down my legs, meowing. He could have been heard as far away as Canterbury. Then he rolled over and went fast asleep. 'I have a problem here,' I thought to myself, 'how on earth am I going to make this sloppy individual do anything interesting?' Finally, he shook himself and got up. At this point, I have to say that I know nothing about animal behaviour, I have never taken degrees in biology, I am simply an emotional painter who loves animals, but I very quickly found out, in a rather unpleasant way, how tigers show they 'love you'. He 'peed' all down my left leg. It seemed like ten minutes because time passes very slowly when hot tiger urine is soaking your left trouser leg and sock! All this time, John was expressing his extreme delight at the fact that Zarif and I had become 'good friends'. He now came in to join me and I explained that I wanted a photograph of a very animated tiger. If I was going to raise a lot of money through a limited edition print of the subject I was painting, it would be useless to portray a tiger fast asleep, with its legs in the air. John pointed out that all his tigers were so friendly: 'I can't make my tigers angry, they are such nice people.' He went on, 'Ah, we haven't fed him for about a week.' My immediate comment on hearing that was, I thought

not unnaturally, 'I wish you'd told me that before I went in to meet him.'

To get an action shot, it was arranged that we would feed a very hungry Zarif with a great chunk of meat and then, after ten minutes when he was settled into his meal, I would get just a few feet away from him and, on a countdown of ten, take a photograph just as John took his lunch away. It didn't work. Zarif was so friendly. He simply asked for his lunch back. Finally, in exasperation, having tried every other method to wake him up, John very gently trod on his front paw. This resulted in the most marvellous snarl which, by good fortune, I managed to catch on film, and I painted *Tiger Fire* from that. The 850 prints sold out in six weeks and raised £127,000. I apologised to Zarif and he understood.

This was perhaps the first real occasion on which I was able to realise just how easily I could repay my debt to wildlife through no effort at all – after all, I would have painted the picture anyway. However, the success of this project created immediate problems. Through the inevitable media interest that it created, it seemed that almost every charity in the country was writing or telephoning me to ask if I would do a similar scheme for them. I had to say no; there is a limit to what one can do in one's spare time. However, there was one exception, to start with anyway.

Lancaster Bomber

The Royal Air Force Benevolent Fund was one of the first charities to approach me after the success of *Tiger Fire*. 'Will you raise the same sort of sum for us?' How could I say no? After all, it was the Royal Air Force in Nairobi that had commissioned my very first wildlife painting. I agreed, but on one condition. For years I had wanted to paint another painting of a Lancaster Bomber, my favourite aeroplane.

The Fund organisers simply said, 'We'll be jolly grateful, whatever aeroplane you paint, as long as it raises lots of money.' However, there was more to it than this. I could see in my scheming mind that there might be a chance of actually flying in PA474, one of only two Lancasters in the world that were still flying, out of more than 7,000 built. I pointed out to the Fund that I believed it was essential 'to fly in an aeroplane, in order to paint a picture of it'. (Which is not actually true.) The reply that came back was disappointing: 'Sorry, David. If we let you fly in it, we shall have to say yes to everybody else.'

I don't give up that easily. A few days later, I contacted the Royal Air Force Battle of Britain Memorial Flight who look after the Lancaster. I spoke to their chief pilot and, once again, it is not 'what you know, but who you know'.

'Of course, David. No problem. We are flying up next week to a Lancaster Squadron reunion in the north-east. You can come with us and sit up in the mid-upper turret.'

I was in my element, returning to my boyhood, holding the mock guns and pretending to shoot German aeroplanes down in the Battle of Britain, as the Spitfire on one side and the Hurricane on the other zoomed in so close I could see the pilots' faces.

When I actually did the painting, I did not want to use photographs, of which there are many, taken during the war, and which are now in the files of the Imperial War Museum. So we decided to recreate the scene at Conningsby, the home of the Battle of Britain Memorial Flight. We gathered together all the appropriate equipment: motorcycles, bicycles, staff cars and fuelling bowsers, of the period. One authentic vehicle was actually towed out of a farmer's field; he was using it to feed his pigs. All those who loaned their vehicles were put up in the Officers' Mess as guests of the Royal Air Force. Some of the owners had driven a long way just for the excitement of taking part in the project. We had a

On the Ark.

marvellous and entertaining five days moving everything around to suit my camera. Although Conningsby was a front-line fighter station, we even managed to get the crash tender to come over and flood the runway below the Lancaster with 2,000 gallons of water to give the effect of a recent rain shower.

I decided to publish a limited edition of 850 signed and numbered copies. For the added bonus to the Fund of a surcharge on some of the prints, the buyer would obtain the signatures of Dr Barnes Wallis, of 'bouncing bomb' fame, and Air Chief Marshal Sir Arthur 'Bomber' Harris. One hundred and eighty people took up this offer and I had the privilege and thrill of spending a day with each of these two great gentlemen. This whole project inevitably rekindled so many World War II memories of my boyhood. On the day that I had flown in the Lancaster, I was allowed to go into her hangar on my own in the late evening. The Lancaster was standing under one dim light hanging from the roof and her four Merlin engines were still ticking; at that moment, I could well understand why those who flew Lancasters in the war had such a deep affection for this fine aircraft.

These strong feelings manifested themselves in an even more unusual way. When the news got around that

there were going to be prints available of my painting, I received two letters within a week of each other, from two total strangers. Both were World War II Lancaster pilots, long since retired; both wanted to buy a print and each letter said virtually the same thing. In one, 'I have heard about the print. I'll only buy it if it's M for Mother. She was my Lancaster. She got me back from Cologne on one engine. I don't want any other aeroplane.' The other one said, 'D for Dog was my Lancaster. She brought me back on three engines from Hamburg. No other Lancaster matters.' I had foreseen this problem arising, having done so many paintings for the three Services, so I had cunningly placed one of the vehicles in the painting in front of the identification letter on the side of the fuselage, making PA474 an 'anonymous' aeroplane. They each bought a print!

The print, by the way, raised £96,000 for the Royal Air Force Benevolent Fund. It is such fun raising money for charities in this way. One is inevitably thanked, but the thanks should come from me; I enjoyed having the excuse to paint a picture of my favourite aeroplane, and actually fly in it. If you can raise £96,000 into the bargain, then what could be better? I still have the original. It means so much to me, I could never part with it.

The Royal Navy and HMS *Ark Royal*

The charity telephones started ringing even louder after the success of the Lancaster print, *Winter of '43 Somewhere in England*. It was the Royal Navy next. They had read of the success of *Tiger Fire* and the Lancaster project and they asked me if I could raise funds for the Fleet Air Arm Museum at Yeovilton in Somerset. Anyone reading this will no doubt have guessed by now that I enjoy playing around with 'Big Things'. In 1978, you could not get much bigger than 50,000 tons plus of Her Majesty's aircraft carrier, HMS *Ark Royal*. I thought to myself, 'Ah, what a marvellous opportunity to "play" with the *Ark* before she goes to the scrapyard.' The Navy flew me out to Malta and I joined the great ship on her last journey home.

The excitement of the eight days I spent on that great ship was almost too much to bear – some of the most exciting moments of my whole life. The hustle and bustle on the flight deck of a great aircraft carrier, such as the *Ark*, at sea, is fantastic. Every few minutes, it seemed, Buccaneers and Phantoms were being catapulted off the end of the flight deck, and Gannets, with their wings folded like prehistoric insects, were coming around the corner. I really had to behave myself and listen to the strict safety instructions given to me because I believe the

Navy had been warned that I am inclined to get carried away with excitement to the point where I might do something stupid; and to do something stupid on the flight-deck would be highly dangerous.

I spent most of the eight days up in the air in the air-sea rescue helicopter, which had to be 'on station' when aircraft were catapulting, in case of a 'ditching' into the sea. This was a marvellous opportunity to take dozens of photographs of the ship at all different angles as she sailed serenely through a calm Mediterranean below me. The only problem was that I suffered from the most appalling vertigo. I always used to be OK in the early days, but due to flying with the Army in helicopters without doors on, and other precarious situations that I had found myself in over the years, I had by now reached the stage where I could hardly drive over the Severn Bridge without gripping the steering wheel! The operator opened the doors of the Wessex helicopter so that I could get a better view; it didn't help my peace of mind very much to be told, 'If you fall out, there is no problem, you have a harness on and we'll pull you back up again.'

Thinking about all this excitement after all this time, I feel slightly guilty at the way I behaved. I was like a small boy with a new toy. When I was in the helicopter, I was able to talk, via the pilot of the helicopter, directly to Ted, Captain Anson, of the *Ark Royal*, sailing below me. I began to realise that if, for example, I asked him to turn just a few degrees to starboard, it would give me a choice of shadows on the ship. After eight days I was getting rather carried away with all the fun of it. 'Ted, I am sorry. The sun is in the wrong position at the moment. Do you think you could turn right round and go back to Malta

again?' A few minutes later, the great ship did exactly that, just for me. What a feeling of power! (And I wasn't even in the Navy.)

Because HMS *Ark Royal* was on her last journey home, there was considerable media interest. When we left Malta, we had teams from both the BBC and ITN on board, together with the First Sea Lord. Filming and interviewing was going on all the time for what would no doubt have made interesting and topical pieces for the television news. There was plenty of good material for the cameras. I was on board when, for example, the very last deck landing of a fixed-wing aircraft onto a fleet aircraft carrier of the Royal Navy took place; it was the end of some fifty years of naval aviation in this form. However, one event killed the whole story. The ship's company decided that the wardroom piano, which had originally been stolen from the Royal Air Force anyway, had come to the end of its useful life. It was decided to give it a formal burial at sea and what I was about to witness was so emotional that I believe almost the entire crew of HMS *Ark Royal* had tears in their eyes. The piano was brought up on the lift from below, with a guard of honour of Royal Marines in No 1 dress uniform. The military band was playing the 'Dead March from Saul' as the pallbearers ceremoniously carried the piano on to the catapult. Then, to more solemn music and a formal salute from the captain and the officers, the catapult sent the piano flying into the Mediterranean to be lost forever in the deep. Only the British could do this sort of thing, and do it properly. It made me feel madly patriotic! By this time, the Russian 'spy ships' which always shadowed the *Ark* had gone away. They knew all about her 'secrets'. I wonder what

they would have thought about a piano going overboard – a new secret weapon, perhaps!

On leaving the great ship to be flown home, I apologised to Ted for being a nuisance. 'That's OK, David,' came the reply, 'By asking me to turn around in circles occasionally, it gave the navigator something to do instead of going back to England in a straight line.'

On my arrival in England, we all watched the television news. All we saw was the piano; the First Sea Lord, and all the other interviews, had been cut!

In order to obtain absolute accuracy in the painting, quite apart from the detail on the flight deck itself, I wanted to see the form that the bow wave would take when a carrier was going fast; HMS *Ark Royal* was not going fast enough when I saw her. I felt I had to get these things correct and the Navy pulled out all the stops for me. It happened that HMS *Bulwark*, a Commando carrier, was about to sail to the United States from Plymouth. I was told that if I was prepared to spend just the first night and day on board, they would demonstrate what a bow wave looked like when a carrier was going fast. The next day, when HMS *Bulwark* was in Mounts Bay, I flew up in a helicopter and the old girl was pushed to the limit, sailing round in circles especially for me and creating the most marvellous effect. It was just what I wanted, and I put HMS *Bulwark*'s bow wave into the painting of HMS *Ark Royal* – not many people know that! (I shudder to think what the poor 'stokers' thought of me!)

The limited edition print of HMS *Ark Royal* raised a very worthwhile sum for a good cause. Tigers, Lancaster Bombers and aircraft carriers have all played a part in my exciting life.

'THIS IS YOUR LIFE'

I WAS AT THE National Exhibition Centre in Birmingham when Michael Aspel presented me with his red book saying, 'David Shepherd, this is your life.' It was a shock, I nearly collapsed on the floor, in front of a lot of people, too.

Avril and I always go for the first two days of the Spring Fair at the NEC in early February. This is a vast trade show covering all aspects of fancy goods, in printing, publishing, and framing. My publishers, in common with other fine art print publishers, have a stand on which they display new works from their artists

that will be published in the forthcoming months. I show three or four brand new paintings which are, hopefully, greeted with anticipation from those gallery owners who support me by buying my prints.

We set the alarm for 6 o'clock in the morning, and then drive up to Euston where we leave the car in an obscure lay-by. We then hop on the train and come back by the same method the next day. On this particular occasion, the alarm went as planned and my wife rushed into the bathroom. As this is appearing in print, I will not go into too many details, but I realised later that she is obvi-

ously a far better actress than I could ever have imagined. She staggered back into bed. 'Darling, I have got a terrible virus and headache. I won't be able to make it.' I confess that I can be very intolerant in such circumstances – I love going with her to the NEC and the thought of going on my own put me into one of my worst moods, particularly at that early hour. 'Get the doctor, then,' I retorted and left the house in a foul temper. The moment I was out of the door, she was out of bed, perfectly fit, and on the telephone to Thames Television. 'He's on his way.'

Of course, Avril was in on the secret; she had been for

Me and my girls – Mandy, Melanie, Wendy and Melinda. (Studio Cole Ltd)

four months. Thames Television probe into the deepest corners of your early life when you are going to be the victim of 'This is Your Life'. They obviously go to one's nearest and dearest and for those four months, Avril had been in connivance with the researchers, and I had never found out. My secretary of the time was never told; she might have let out the secret (if the 'victim' finds out, even the very day before he is going to be 'captured', they cancel the programme. It has to be an absolute surprise, not only to the victim, but to the viewing audience on television). I will believe anything I am told. Avril kept telling me that she was 'going up to London to buy a new hat from Harrods'. I believed her for some incredible reason; if I had thought for a second, I would have realised that she hardly ever wears a hat, and she hardly ever goes to Harrods!

I drove up to London and left the car in a side street near Euston Station. I bought a return ticket to Birmingham and arrived at the NEC. When I came on the stand, there were great crowds of people milling around, many of them friends. I also noticed a television camera set up ready to film me, but this was all part of the clever plot worked out down to the finest detail. It happened that ITV and myself were in the final process of putting together a documentary for the series 'Nature Watch', and they pointed out that this was an ideal opportunity to have me talk to camera about a few more details of my painting life. It never occurred to me that it was anyone else. It was a marvellous cover-up and as the cameras started running and I began chatting about painting elephants, Michael Aspel suddenly appeared from round the corner holding something behind his back. The real reason for his presence still never occurred to me. I said,

'Hello Michael, fancy seeing you again. What are you doing here?' I then noticed that he was holding a microphone. He realised that he could no longer carry on the confidence trick and at that moment said, 'David Shepherd, this is your life.' Most of the audience around me knew what was going on. It was a magical moment as, greeted with cheers, I very nearly collapsed on to my knees with shock. (That is what is meant to happen.)

'We're flying back to Heathrow, David.' This was the second shock. 'What do I do about my return ticket on British Rail? What about my car?'

The research team for 'This is Your Life' can only be likened to the KGB (in the nicest way) such is the subterfuge that goes on. 'You can throw your ticket away for a start. We are driving your car back to your home in Surrey.' I wondered how. I had parked it, as usual, in the obscure lay-by. But they had actually followed me and seen me park. 'How are you going to drive my car back if I have got the keys?' 'You have not got the keys. We have.' They had stolen them out of my jacket pocket!

Perhaps people don't realise that, such is the popularity of this long-running programme, if the 'victim' is seen with Michael Aspel, the general public can then very well guess who he may be, a month later when the programme is actually on the television screen. My face is not well known in any way. Nevertheless, to make absolutely certain that the secret was safe in front of the travelling public, I was at one end of the aeroplane and Michael was at the other. I was sitting next to one of the researchers on the aircraft and, still believing that Avril was ill, I said 'How on earth are you going to go ahead with the programme if my wife's ill in bed?' 'We've made arrangements' was the guarded and unhelpful reply. Was she going to be brought in on a stretcher? Of course not, she was perfectly OK – as I have said. I am so gullible!

An hour or so after landing at Heathrow, I came on to the stage at Teddington Studios and was confronted by some hundred of our friends, all of whom had been let into the secret, together with lots of people who sit in the audience to see the show. Right from the start, I was so emotional I could hardly speak. Avril obviously came in first, hail and hearty, and sat beside me. Then, one by one, friends who I had not seen for years, or who had played a significant part in my life, came on the set. For example, I met after sixty years, the editor of Nursery World. It was in that magazine that I had coloured the outline of a tiger when I was eleven years old, and won the first prize. Peter Mumford came on. He was the man who had taken pity on me when I was on my beam ends in Kenya, and given me the job for £1 a week at the Sindbad Hotel in Malindi. The late and much missed Bill

Travers came on with his wife, Virginia McKenna. Then, Robin Goodwin; the programme would not have been the same without him.

Perhaps the most moving thing of all was the fact that the researchers had flown over to Hollywood and interviewed James Stewart in Beverley Hills. Avril and I and the family had known Jimmy for many years. He had stayed with us for a weekend in our farmhouse in Surrey and we had formed a very close friendship.

The team flew to Zambia to interview the President, Dr Kenneth Kaunda; and Prince Bernhard of the Netherlands, another very close and dear friend, then said some flattering things about me. He was followed by His Royal Highness Prince Michael of Kent, who is the patron of the David Shepherd Conservation Foundation. That was the moment when Michael Aspel said 'You've certainly got some posh friends.' By this time, I was almost helpless with emotion.

I had noticed that there was one empty seat at the end of the row, next to three of our four daughters. Could this empty seat be for our youngest daughter, Wendy, who might be flying from America? I did at least guess that much but there was more. It happened that just before the programme was going to be televised, Avril and I were spending a day in London. She told Thames Television this and they took the opportunity to prepare another surprise for me. The whole team came down to the studio and they put a sheet on the floor. They then marked the positions of all my easels with chalk; they don't miss a trick. (I might have noticed that everything had been moved on returning in the evening.) They then gathered all our grandchildren together and invited them to paint elephants in my studio. As a climax to the programme, all the little ones came on to the set holding their artistic efforts, to the cheers of the audience. They were accompanied by our youngest daughter, Wendy, who had been flown from Wyoming with her husband.

Somehow, Avril had managed to inform nearly a hundred of our closest friends, without me knowing, and they sat in the audience. At the end of the programme, Michael Aspel and the team invited us to join them for dinner in the Studios and this went on until 2 o'clock in the morning. It was the most marvellously happy evening and they really pulled out all the stops for us; we were treated like VIPs.

One amusing moment completes the story. Just as we were leaving for dinner, I heard one member of the public say to another as she was getting into her car, 'It was quite a good programme, I suppose. He was quite a decent sort of bloke, but I still don't know who the hell he was.'

ON FILM

BEING AN UNASHAMED extrovert, I quite openly admit that I love being in front of a TV camera. Quite apart from the fun that I have had over the years, it is also so worthwhile if, through the all-powerful medium of television, we can bring home the now so desperate issues, such as saving the tiger, the rhino, the mountain gorillas of Rwanda, and the elephant.

The Man Who Loves Giants

My first venture into filming was with the BBC Natural History Unit. It was in 1971 that they decided to film my crazy life with elephants, steam engines, and nuclear bombers, for a fifty-minute documentary, *The Man Who Loves Giants*. A tremendous number of people must have seen the film then, and in the years since, all over the world, and its success was no doubt very largely due to the fact that we were able to obtain the services of our friend James Stewart. Jimmy is a great conservationist and his famous voice lent just the right note to the film's commentary.

We had six intensive weeks filming together in Africa, America, and all over Britain and never a cross word passed between us. Indeed, we had hilarious times together on the project.

One of the earliest locations was in America when I took some five or six paintings out to be auctioned. These, together with many gifts given to us by other generous artists, enabled us to raise, in twenty minutes, the money necessary to buy the Bell Jet Ranger helicopter that we presented to President Kaunda of Zambia for anti-poaching work in Zambia's National Parks.

We then went to Royal Air Force, Marham, where, as I have already described in an earlier chapter, I was commissioned to paint the night-flight refuelling exercise in a Valiant, and we got some spectacular footage. At that time, the bombers were very much on the protected list and the film had to be passed by the Ministry of Defence, just in case we were giving secrets away to the Russians!

While at Marham, we took the opportunity to recreate the days in the early 1950s when I began my career at London Airport (Heathrow) painting Constellations and Stratocruisers. The illusion was remarkably successful. I always painted in a howling gale at Heathrow, and the easel, as I have already described, often had to be weighed down with bricks. Inevitably, on the very day that we wanted to recreate this scene at Marham, there wasn't a breath of wind. We had to ask the station commander to lend us his Chipmunk light aircraft to create a wind! While I was filmed painting, he sat in the cockpit and revved up the engine so much that I was practically blown off the airfield; but we got the desired effect.

I was particularly delighted when the BBC agreed that we should incorporate a sequence featuring my portrait of Christ in the Army church at Bordon. We filmed a Sunday morning service and I think the little church had never been so full. Of the very considerable number of letters I received after the screening of the film, the majority made particular reference to this sequence. Incidentally, that one painting, which, as I have stated, I would love to be remembered by, has created much interest from the few people who know about it. (I was on Roy Plumley's 'Desert Island Discs' many years ago talking about the painting and again it generated more comment than anything else.)

To incorporate my 'steam engine love affair', we filmed some hilarious footage of myself, clad in oil-covered overalls, struggling to lift heavy spare parts out of derelict engines at Barry scrapyard in Glamorgan, with my 'mates'. One of the more colourful of my helpers in the film was Steve, a Geordie, who, on occasions, used the sort of language that was most certainly not appropriate for a family film. Steve was never happier than when he was covered from head to foot in oil and muck. At the request of the director, he disappeared into the bowels of one of the wrecks in the scrapyard, from which we were hoping to obtain spares. At the instructions, 'Roll the camera' I was supposed to ask Steve, 'What's it like in there, Steve?' Steve was to pop up from inside the engine and make some appropriate comment. Nothing was rehearsed and the cameras rolled. I asked the question. Steve forgot that he was being filmed – his reply was totally unrepeatable. 'Steve, this is a family show. Please calm your language down.' We had to take this sequence five times before we managed to persuade him to say, 'Oh, it's very filthy.' When we saw the film, we could hardly realise that it was Steve – he never spoke like that!

Next, we moved to Africa for three weeks where we filmed on the Zambezi Sawmills Railway, the Victoria Falls, and then down to Germiston steam sheds outside Johannesburg. We obtained what must now be quite historic footage of that great steam shed. At that time, there must have been nearly two hundred giant locomotives in steam. I set my easel up outside the sheds, surrounded by enormous South African Railways locomotives, shunting and moving off in all directions, pouring smoke into the air, and so much was happening I hardly knew where to look. I was so excited. Jimmy Stewart said, 'It's just like a small boy left alone in a candy store.'

We then moved off into my beloved Luangwa Valley in Zambia where we got some marvellous footage of me painting from life in the bush. At one point, the director wanted to include an elephant sequence and he said, 'How about filming you walking up to some elephants and painting them?'

'Don't be so stupid. No one has ever been crazy enough to do that.'

'Well, you'd probably be mad enough, David, so let's have a go.'

It was that marvellously British 'stiff upper lip' spirit all over again – we will probably all get killed, but won't it be fun?

I suppose it must seem a bit daft for an artist to approach two bull elephants to within sixty paces (about six for an elephant), carrying his studio easel and a very large canvas, sixteen tubes of oil paint, a palette, brushes, and linseed oil; then set everything up and expect the elephants to stand still while their portraits are being painted.

We were quite a crowd. We needed two Land Rovers and we all piled in and drove off into the park. It was a hot day and, eventually, we saw two lovely bull elephants minding their own business under a tree, fanning themselves in the heat of midday. We got out and prepared all our equipment.

Elephants have extremely poor eyesight, but a very acute sense of smell and good hearing. First, we had to test the wind; if the elephants had suspected anything, they would have gone in an instant. The wind was absolutely reliable and in our favour. Silence was also essential and we now proceeded to walk as quietly as possible, in a long line, up to the two completely unsuspecting elephants.

If some tourists had come round the corner in another Land Rover at that moment, they would have thought that everybody in Zambia was completely out of their minds. They would have seen an artist carrying an easel above his head – if the legs had got caught up in the bushes it might have made a noise which would have woken the elephants up – followed by the director, a programme secretary with notes, a cameraman with a camera and a tripod, a sound recordist with microphone and recording equipment, a couple of game wardens, my wife, and a couple of other guys. It would perhaps have reminded our fellow tourists of the old 'pack train' days of old, walking into unexplored territory with a whole team of porters. This was different because two large elephants were still standing under the tree, just a few paces away.

Finally, when we were almost on top of the elephants, Rolf Rohwer, who at that time was a professional hunter and a great friend of ours, decided that was close enough. By sign language, because we were far too close to speak even in whispers, he indicated that I should start painting. All that could be heard was the gentle whirring of the movie camera behind me. I was quietly in fits of giggles to myself because the whole situation seemed so hysterically unreal. We obtained some excellent and remarkable footage.

The next day, we had another try and it was a very different story. Again, we followed the same procedure, but this time it was a cow elephant, and we realised afterwards that she may have lost her calf or been shot at by poachers. All I remember was the sudden exclamation from Rolf by my side, 'Leave your easel and run, she's coming!' I dropped my brushes and palette, turned round and nearly knocked Avril over. We both picked ourselves up and, giggling like mad, ran back to the Land Rovers as fast as our legs would carry us. I looked over my shoulder and watched the elephant charge, like a tank, past my very lonely-looking easel, straight for Rolf. He stood his ground. That's why he was there, to look after us in just such a potential emergency.

Rolf believes in shouting. He can use pretty foul-mouthed language in such a situation and I believe that cow elephant spoke perfect English. I swear to this day that I saw an expression of absolute horror on her face at the torrent of filthy language that emanated from him and she stopped dead in her tracks in disgust.

From his long experience, Rolf knew that if he had run away, it would have been a complete waste of time – elephants are big animals and they can run very fast. He also knew that he would only shoot her as an absolute

last resort. He loves elephants as much as I do and neither of us would ever have forgiven ourselves if we had had to kill an elephant just for me to be filmed in front of a television camera.

On returning to the Land Rovers, I was shaking with excitement and laughter; I think I even said, 'I wish it would do it again.' Rolf is one of my closest friends, but he didn't think this was very funny. He quite rightly gave me some stern advice: 'David, you will learn one day. I know you love elephants, but you cannot take liberties with them. Next time you come to Zambia, I'll get you really scared.' I have gone back many times since and it hasn't happened yet. Moreover, I don't think I have ever learned, either. I still take liberties and one day I shall probably get a fright, which I well deserve.

Round the camp fire in the evening, when all the excitement of the day was over, we sat talking, as one does in Africa, about lots of things. We inevitably got on to the subject of tourists. Both Rolf and I have enough funny stories about tourists to fill a book. I asked him what I would have done if I had been on my own and had been chased by that cow elephant with no one to protect me. He said, 'You would have climbed the first tree you could find.' I pointed out that I had never climbed a tree in my life. Rolf said, 'You would be amazed, David, what you can do when you have got a four-ton elephant chasing you.' We then had a few more beers and started talking about geriatric ladies from Texas who can't even walk, but, with an elephant after them, they find themselves at the top of the tallest tree they can find in seconds. He was exaggerating, but I got the point.

In Search of Wildlife

It was in 1987 that I was asked by a London documentary film company to feature in six half-hour films on endangered species and this began an episode of my life that has not only led to some enormously exciting experiences, but has also opened up whole new horizons for me, as a painter and also as a conservationist. The series was entitled *In Search of Wildlife* and the films were immediately sold to Thames Television who showed them at peak viewing time. They were subsequently sold to several other countries as well as the United States.

The films were remarkably well received by the critics and achieved very high ratings. I believe one of the reasons for this was that they were different. First of all, I was painting the landscape and the animals concerned in each film, and painting, being highly visual, is perhaps ideal for television. Moreover, I was the person who was learning. I have said many times that I am in no way an

ecologist and in each of the films I was with an expert who was telling me all about the particular species we were featuring.

The films were also different in so far as virtually all the dialogue was completely unprepared with no script and all was done on location. I think that the six films gained from this spontaneity, but it created fearful problems for the producer. Whenever I saw anything new or exciting, I got carried away with the exhilaration of it all and I was then almost impossible to film!

The first film took us to the beautiful Yellowstone National Park in the USA. This was my first venture into painting North American wildlife and to many people, the main feature of the Yellowstone Park are the bison. I could hardly believe it when I first saw them. They all appeared to be having a 'sauna'. The geysers, for which the park is so famous, belch sulphurous fumes and clouds of steam and bubbles from the ground and, standing right in the middle of it, apparently enjoying themselves, was a small group of bison.

In complete contrast, we then moved up to Churchill, a bleak fishing port on the southern shores of Hudson Bay in northern Manitoba. On arrival, my first feeling was that I wondered why anybody would want to live there, let alone visit the place. It is in fact a grain terminal, but only when the Gulf of St Lawrence is open, in the summer. Otherwise, the whole place is ice-bound and the town is totally cut off from the outside world except by air or by rail. Nevertheless, there is a major attraction that draws tourists in their hundreds to Churchill from all over the world – the polar bears.

During the summer, the bears produce their cubs, inland from Churchill. In the autumn, they begin to trek back onto the ice for the winter where, feeding on their natural diet of seals, they can regain the weight and condition lost during the summer months. While in Churchill, they stop over to eat. Like all places inhabited by man, the garbage from the town has to be dumped somewhere and it is Churchill's rubbish tips that attract the polar bears. They are drawn, among other things, to the oil in foam rubber and other trash, and it is the most amazing sight to see them nibbling at the seats of old wrecked cars. For years now, this has all been going on within yards of children going to school; neither take any notice of the other. However, the Canadian authorities have always had the fear that someone would eventually get hurt, so the bears are caught in traps, humanely, and then taken out on to the ice by helicopters and put where they belong. Hopefully, they get the message and do not come back into the town again – though some inevitably do just that.

Nowadays, the bears do seem to have learnt their lesson, and very few get caught, but we were incredibly lucky – the first trap we came to had a bear in it. The traps consist of railway sleepers piled on top of each other to a height of about one and a half metres (some 4–5ft) in the form of a 'V'. Meat is put inside the trap at the 'sharp end'. The bear, attracted by the smell of the meat, steps into the wide end of the trap. In doing so he puts his foot on a spring which clamps him by the leg, but the amazing thing is that it causes him no damage or pain. Unlike almost any other animal which, when caught in a trap, would thrash around furiously, the bears don't seem to mind. When we arrived at the trap, the bear was simply sitting with his chin on the edge as if to say, 'Would you please do something about this?'

The bear was tranquillised and, when it was 'out cold', it was tagged with a number on its ear and various other procedures were carried out. It was then very gently lifted on to a truck and we drove back into the town to the 'Polar Bear Jail'. Any bears that are caught are kept in complete seclusion and quiet for up to two weeks, completely away from human contact. No one at all is allowed into the cell and I was told by the ecologist with us that the bears are quite calm and undisturbed by this treatment. At the end of the period they are taken out of the jail, slung beneath a helicopter and flown out on to the ice.

After filming all of these sequences in the town, we went out into the arctic wastes of the tundra in a 'tundra-buggy'. These are buses especially converted with enormous wheels to get them over the barren landscape. Again, we were lucky. The sun came out for about a quarter of a minute only – the only time it did all the time we were in Churchill – and we saw a wild polar bear.

It was an amazing experience to get out of the bus and walk very quietly and slowly up to within a few dozen paces of him. A number of people who have seen the film have said to me, 'You must have been tremendously brave.' It was not a question of being brave, it was just a question of being sensible. The polar bear knew I was there and the ecologist with me told me just how far I could go. I was so cold that it was almost impossible even to hold my sketch block, but we ended up with some very interesting film.

Next, we went to India for tigers, at Ranthambhore National Park, near Jaipur. Here, I found a park which, for sheer spectacle, could actually compete with my beloved Luangwa Valley in Zambia. Indeed, I would go further; Ranthambhore is perhaps one of the most beautiful places I will ever visit. Not only is it four hundred square kilometres (150sq miles) of glorious and lush vegetation, and beautiful hills and lakes, but another bonus, it is 'tiger city'. Ranthambhore reminded me so strongly of Rudyard Kipling's *Jungle Book*, for here, in the jungle, entwined by great trees twisting their roots in and out of the stone, are ruined temples dating back some three or four hundred years, built by the Mogul emperors for their harems. Shafts of sunlight filtered through the huge trees on to the mosaic swimming pools and shrines and to cap it all, the tigers walk in and out of the ruins. What a subject for an artist!

I visited Ranthambhore in 1991, and within minutes of going into the park on the first afternoon, we found three tigers just calmly lying right on the edge of the road and we approached to within a few feet of them. They took no notice whatsoever. At that time, it was estimated that there were forty-eight tigers in the park; it is now thought that there are fewer than twelve. Some of this is due to mismanagement, but it is mainly because of poaching for their bones, which fetch an enormous price in the Far East. So I was lucky, and we were lucky to film, in one of the most beautiful places on earth.

The next film in the series featured the American alligator, in Florida. There are some success stories in conservation, and this is one of them. The American alligator was on the endangered list; it is now off it. Until a few years ago the illegal importation, from South America into Miami, of skins of wild alligators that had been killed by poachers was on a gigantic scale. We filmed in a contraband store that was filled to the brim with various products from endangered species impounded by the Wildlife Service. Now, ranching and farming of alligators (the skins are tanned and turned into handbags and other goods) has to a very large degree knocked the bottom out of the illegal alligator-skin trade, so the pressure has been taken off those alligators in the wild. This issue made me think a very great deal, especially when I was being filmed by the television team actually in an alligator skin tannery. I would still not buy Avril a handbag made out of crocodile skin, but at least now I am more enlightened and think more deeply of all these issues.

We wanted to see 'gators' and we drove up to Gainsville, in the heart of 'gator country'; the whole town is 'gator crazy'. Motels and restaurants are named after alligators and all the students from the university seemed to be walking around with 'gator T-shirts'. Just outside the town, on a large lake, we spent a day on an airboat, skimming across the water looking for 'gators. 'Gators! The lake was full of them. I had my easel with me and, as the sun began to go down, I painted the scene which, with its floating water lilies and profusion of bird life, was

Painting elephant seals for Thames Television.

quite beautiful. Then, after dark, came the greatest excitement of all. We had lamps on our helmets and we skimmed slowly across the water in the pitch dark. The lights caught the alligators' eyes, which shone like little jewels. We found a nest and I gently put my hand into the water and picked up five little baby alligators about twenty-three centimetres (9in) long in my hand – delightful little people. Sadly, so many people look upon reptiles, such as alligators and crocodiles, as slimy and dangerous. They should experience what I did and they would think again.

One of the six programmes featured the grey whale and for this, we flew to San Francisco. Here, our first location was at a now derelict whaling station, a place full of ghosts and memories of slaughter and dead whales.

We then flew on down to San Diego, where we joined a cruise boat and sailed south down the Californian coast. Our first port of call was a remote island, San Benitos, in San Ignacio Lagoon, off Baja California. San Benitos is a nature reserve put aside entirely for elephant seals and other forms of wildlife. Only a few people are allowed on it, by special permission. We went ashore, watched by dozens of little bobbing heads in the surf. It was a sea-lion colony as well, and I am sure the animals were wondering what on earth was going to happen when they saw an artist leaping out of a boat into the surf, carrying an easel above his head to stop it getting wet!

It would not be exaggerating to say that this bare rocky outcrop was a seething mass of seals and elephant seals, with all the attendant sights and smells, many of them revolting. There was hardly a blade of vegetation anywhere and it was almost impossible to walk without tripping over an animal of some sort. The elephant seals were totally unafraid. These enormous animals weigh up to one and a half tons and they were all around me. I set my easel up and started painting within a few yards of some hundred or so of these gigantic animals looking at me with their dog-like faces and limpid eyes. It was so funny I could hardly paint; one seal actually waddled in between the tripod legs of my easel as I was working. I have painted in crowds before, but this was different!

Just a day's sailing on down the coast and we came to Baja Lagoon. I had never seen a whale in the wild before and I was getting more excited by the minute. The unfortunate programme producer saw his chances of filming me behaving even half sensibly rapidly diminishing by the second.

In our first afternoon there, from an inflatable boat, Avril and I must have seen a hundred of these marvellous animals.

There were six of us in the boat and we spent three days in the lagoon watching whales playing and cavorting in the water. Their great tail flukes were coming out of the water and slapping down onto the surface again. It was altogether a thrilling experience because we felt the whales were happy and doing it just for fun. One sees this sort of thing on television, but there is nothing like seeing it in real life. The great thing about whale watching is the anticipation because one doesn't know where to look; anywhere around us in the lagoon at any moment, a great whale would leap out of the water like an enormous torpedo and crash back again, through, it seemed, sheer exhilaration.

The whales in the lagoon at that time of the year were calving and we saw many mothers with their new-born babies. The researcher with us said, 'David, if we're really lucky, we might get a "friendly".' I had no idea what he meant until he explained that some of the grey whales are exactly that; they come right up to the boat to get to know the people in them.

On the third afternoon we were getting drowsy in the heat and had almost given up hope of seeing a 'friendly'. We only had another couple of hours before we had to leave the lagoon and start the long journey back home, when suddenly the sea erupted about sixty metres (200ft) away. 'We've got one!' The sea went quiet again and then, looking under the water, we watched as a grey whale measuring some twelve and a half metres (40ft) in length, came closer and closer to us, about sixty centimetres (2 feet) below the surface. In my excitement, I nearly upset the boat. I was told to behave myself by the producer as the whole object of this expensive exercise

was to get some sensible film of me, but I could hardly contain myself. The poor sound recordist, lying off-camera in the bottom of the boat with her tape-recorder, was trying without much success to get some audible sense out of me, and I trod on her in my enthusiasm – but she didn't mind too much. All the poor cameraman could do by this time was to point the camera and hope that something would come out; it did. The whale came right up to the boat and its eye was about a metre (3ft) away, looking at me. I stretched my arm over the side of the boat, the underwater camera came with me and captured my hand on film, actually touching the whale.

It was a highly emotional experience. It was much more than just touching the whale, however. I began to think seriously about it the moment it drifted away. How could that wonderful creature with a brain much bigger than ours, allow man, its most implacable enemy, to be so familiar? Like my beloved elephants, I am sure that whales never forget. I am convinced that this animal must have known what we have done to its ancestors – butchered them by the countless thousands in cold blood, for money. Trust is a marvellous thing.

The story of the Arabian oryx is surely one of the great conservation success stories and it was decided that one of the six films must feature this beautiful animal. For years, the Arabs in the empty quarter of Saudi Arabia have hunted down the Arabian oryx because of their traditional belief that in killing one, the hunter will assimilate the grace and speed of his quarry. It is in man's instinct to hunt, and I would never question this. Hunting from camels always gave the oryx a fair chance. However, it was a very different story when, through oil revenue, the people concerned were now able to hunt from Mercedes vehicles with automatic weapons. The result was inevitable. In the early 1960s, the Arabian oryx was on the brink of extinction; some researchers thought that there were just 13 animals left in the wild.

When I was in Aden with the Royal Air Force in 1960, they flew into the interior with a tranquillising team and five animals were drugged and taken to Phoenix Zoo in America. It is said that the remaining animals were almost immediately wiped out by one hunting party, so the animal was rescued at the eleventh hour.

From those original animals taken to the United States, well over three hundred have been bred, not only in Phoenix Zoo, but in San Diego Wildlife Park and we went there first to see the oryx in captivity.

Through the inspiration of the Sultan of Muscat, a programme for the reintroduction of the Arabian oryx into the wild was instigated and this has now been

running for several years. A considerable number of animals have been flown from the United States to Muscat in DC10s. They are then picked up by the Sultan's Air Force and flown to holding pens in the desert.

For the film, we flew to Muscat and then to an incredibly remote place called Jalooni, right out in the desert, to see the operation actually working. We saw the Arabian oryx gradually becoming acclimatised to their natural environment before being released into the wild. Day after day we drove out into the featureless flat desert, a vast gravel plain where it seems almost nothing could possibly live. I was once told that there is a part of this area where it has not rained for twenty-five years. In good times, it probably rains for just a couple of days in the year at the most.

On one particular morning when we were driving out, our American ecologist said, 'David, it's been a marvellous season this year. It's rained so well. Can you see the grazing?'

Grazing? I immediately began thinking of lush green English pastures. I could hardly believe it because, to my untrained eye, in front of us was nothing except desert with a few stunted bushes. Then, when it was pointed out to me and I looked really carefully, I could just detect a little shimmer of green here and there. It had rained some two months previously, and by one of nature's sure miracles, this had generated a minute growth of little desert plants less than two centimetres (1in) high. This was grazing, and the oryx live on it.

When we were filming, there were forty-one Arabian oryx in the wild. The amazing thing is that they are spread over a distance of 9,500 square kilometres (3,700 sq miles). One way of making this point is to suggest that this is the equivalent of three in Berlin, three in Paris, two in Rome, one in London, and five in Birmingham. Each little group is looked after day and night by a group of Bedouin Arabs in their stationwagons. They all have walkie-talkie communications, so the whereabouts of these wandering animals is never unknown.

I had the thrill of being allowed to walk, very, very quietly, in the searing heat, up to within painting distance of eight of these lovely, pure white animals sheltering from the burning sun under a tree. I felt deeply at that moment that I was seeing something very rare indeed. I was even more moved by the knowledge that the Arabs tending these animals with such dedication could well be descendants of the very same people who brought them to the brink of extinction just a few years ago. They now look after them instead of shooting them; that is what conservation means.

CONSERVATION MATTERS

I'VE LEARNED a very great deal since I saw those 255 zebra lying dead on the ground around that poisoned water hole in 1960. I was ignorant in those days. It is a long time ago now, and I hardly knew what conservation meant. I don't think many other people did, either. Of course, I was vaguely familiar with the glossy travel brochures selling holidays to Kenya and elsewhere. Such photographs, in glorious technicolour, show waterholes around which zebra, giraffe and antelope are drinking, at peace with the world. Of course, there are still waterholes like that. But the world has changed and it is changing very fast, for the worse. In 1960, I knew nothing about conservation. However, when I surveyed that grizzly scene, I became a conservationist in one dramatic moment, and it changed my life.

I have already described how, at that same time, my career was rapidly taking off due to the immediate success of my wildlife paintings. Standing around that poisoned waterhole, I would therefore have only been half a person if I had not said to myself there and then, 'If man is capable of doing this to his fellow creatures, I must do something in return'.

I am a very lucky man indeed. Many people take months or years to raise the amount of money that I am able to raise with just a few hours' work through the donation of a wildlife painting. I do not want thanks when I say this; I am simply illustrating how easy it is. I have to paint every day that I can because I am a compulsive artist, so I am not giving anything away.

The more material success that my wildlife paintings have brought me, my wife and my family, the more I have learned and seen, so obviously the motivation to play my part and to put something back into conservation is stronger. Conservation work has many dark moments, and many more of them as the years rush by. However, raising money with such apparent ease also has its lighter moments. On one occasion, I was asked to do a painting to raise money at an event in Guildford and the pressure was such that, in the afternoon of the evening in question, I was only able to produce a painting measuring 15 x 15cm (6 x 6in). Moreover, I could not attend because I had already committed myself to another event, but the painting arrived in time, soaking wet and suitably framed. The picture had taken only two hours to paint and I learned afterwards that it had raised

£11,000. Later on, I discovered who the generous man was. The purchaser was a fruit salesman, with an open-air market stall. Wanting to thank him, I happened to be in the area some weeks later, so I queued up with all the other customers who were buying strawberries and bananas from his stall, awaiting my turn. When it arrived, I put my hand across the fruit and said, 'Charlie, I just want to thank you for being so tremendously generous the other night in Guildford. I am David Shepherd, and I want to thank you for giving £11,000 towards wildlife conservation and for my little painting.' His reply was immediate. 'Oh, that's all right, mate. I sold the painting at a profit to somebody else the next morning. Next please!' Raising money can be fun; I meet such a diversity of people!

I am not an ecologist in the true scientific meaning of the word. I have no degrees attached to my name. However, I am very emotional by nature and, as an artist who owes all his success to the animals he paints, I have wept openly and freely in the back of a Land Rover when I have seen elephants dying from suppurating wounds caused by AK47 automatic weapons. Since 1960, I have been privileged to meet, know, and go into the wild with ecologists who know infinitely more than I do about the subjects which we share with such passion - conservation of the environment and wildlife. I have learned a great deal from these marvellous people and I have had many experiences. It is no longer possible to shock me; there seems to be no limit to the depths of depravity to which man can sink.

I have witnessed unbelievable brutality in many parts of the world. Many years ago, I was invited as an independent observer to see the seal hunt in Canada. Readers should note that I do not use the word 'cull' because it is not a cull; it is a hunt, for money. It was in the days when the slaughter was at its worst. With the backing of the Canadian government, up to 200,000 baby seals were bludgeoned to death with clubs in a space of some three weeks. The Canadians have always tried to justify the slaughter as an essential part of their economy; in fact, just a handful of fishermen have benefited. In that particular year, nature had played a trick because it was an exceptionally warm winter throughout the Gulf of St Lawrence and most of the ice-flows on which the pregnant seals would normally have had their

young, far out of the sight of land, had not formed. What ice there was had come ashore onto Prince Edward Island, from which I witnessed the slaughter. I was one of some sixty observers from various welfare organisations throughout the world; a large number of television and media teams were there also because, by now, the strength of revulsion against this barbaric practice was worldwide.

All hell was let loose on that particular morning. Without any control whatsoever, people, young and old, from the town, rushed out onto the ice-flows from the beach and started clubbing the baby seals. I heard one teenager refer to a five-day-old baby white-coat fur seal as a '$20 bill'. From the shores of a national park, I watched as 3,000 five-day-old baby fur seals were hit on the head with clubs and skinned, some of them before they were dead. The sea was running red with blood, and the sickening butchery reached such proportions that, eventually, it had to be called off by the local authorities as a result of pressure from the observers and the media.

I was standing on the beach with a friend who was photographing the slaughter. There was nothing illegal about this, because we were in a national park. Suddenly, however, a Royal Canadian Mounted Police patrol car stormed up behind us and one of the officers ran down to the beach and snatched my friend's camera out of her hands. 'Photography is not allowed here,' he said. Our protests were to no avail and he ripped the film out of the camera. I was so angry that we both agreed that we should consider taking out a charge of assault against the officer concerned. I am not suggesting that all Royal Canadian Police officers behave in this way, although their actions were quite different from the romantic image I had of them, riding into the sunset on horseback! I put the unpleasant incident down to the tension and strength of feeling caused by what was taking place. Shortly after this, the hunt was called off by the local authorities as a result of pressure from the observers and the many television teams filming the butchery.

A group of us decided to get away from all the tension and drive down the coast to see baby seals in peaceful surroundings. It was a great thrill to walk out onto the ice in the crisp air, and there was not a breath of wind;

the silence was almost deafening. My friend and I struggled over the ice-flows until, in front of us, we found a baby seal looking up at us with its limpid eyes. It was totally unafraid because it had never seen humans before and it allowed me to get very close to photograph it. It was an emotional moment and in strong contrast to what was happening a few miles up the coast.

We drove back into the town to find all the fishermen leaving the village hall in a very angry mood. They had been told to stop the seal slaughter because of the glare of publicity from the media. We decided to get out quickly and drove into what we thought was a side turning, but which was, in fact, a cul-de-sac. We were trapped and the fishermen saw us. We were surrounded by a howling mob who promptly slashed all our tyres and threatened us with violence if we got out of the vehicle. After half-an-hour of this terrifying treatment, I noticed a Royal Canadian Mounted Police patrol car coming up the street. I wound the window down furiously and beckoned the car to come alongside. Asking for an immediate escort out of the town, the policeman in the car then recognised me. He asked 'Aren't you David Shepherd? Aren't you the guy who is threatening to take out a prosecution against us?' 'Yes, I am, for assault,' I replied. 'If you withdraw the charge, we will give you an escort'. I could hardly believe it; it seemed horribly like a bribe. I protested strongly and, grudgingly, they escorted us out of the town for a few miles. Then, after leaving us, I noticed that we were being followed by three trucks full of fishermen, but we were allowed to leave peacefully. Those few moments brought home to me just how feelings can rise to fever pitch when it comes to controversial conservation issues. I was certainly still in a state of shock when I arrived back at Heathrow Airport the next day to be interviewed by Kate Adie; I don't think I made a great deal of sense.

Shortly after my return from Prince Edward Island, I was invited onto local radio to talk about the seal slaughter with a representative from the Canadian High Commission. The gentleman was so plausible that he almost convinced me that baby seals enjoyed having their heads bashed in: it made good radio because we had a very heated argument. The remark he made which irritated me most was his contention that seals had to be killed because 'they were eating up all the fish'. I pointed out strongly that it was not the seals that were doing this. It was man who was emptying all the oceans of their marine life without any thought whatsoever for the future.

One of the greatest threats to the whole environment of Africa and elsewhere in the world is the destruction of

At work.

the world's forests for timber by big corporations, a practice which, in certain countries, has reached terrifying proportions. It is possible to look into the future and see nothing but desert in areas which were once covered in lush forest. In an effort to bring this potential disaster home to those who matter, the local people, I tell the story of a certain tree in Zambia. I knew that tree well. It was a huge acacia tree, standing on the main road up to the copper belt, just outside Lusaka. It gets very hot in Zambia in October. Temperatures can reach 36°C (98°F) or more and, while waiting for the bus that usually arrives several hours late, a great crowd of Africans could shelter under the tree's spreading branches from the blazing heat of the sun - a natural bus shelter. This beautiful tree was then hacked down, leaving a 1m (3ft) high tortured stump. Why did they do this? They wanted to use the timber from the tree to build a bus shelter. Now, only a few people are able to shelter from the sun. Men can be very stupid.

One of the joys of my life is to find that so many Africans throughout the Third World are now so responsive and ready to listen, but ignorance is a frightening thing. Living as I do in leafy Surrey, I am sickened at times at the attitude expressed by certain people who, because they have been to Tangier for a holiday, 'know all about Africa'. I have had some very offensive things said to me by such people - for example, 'Now Zambia has become independent, I suppose they will kill all the animals'. In fact, when Northern Rhodesia became Zambia in 1964, there was just one national park. There are now nineteen. Surely that speaks for itself.

After so many years of experience since I saw those dead zebra in 1960, I have begun to wonder if it is all really worth it. I have become more and more of a pessimist. Conservation does not start and stop in Africa. In our own sceptred isle, we are still ripping out 4,800km (3,000 miles) of hedgerow every year. Since I became a conservationist, therefore, nearly 161,000km (100,000 miles) of hedgerow have disappeared under the blades of the bulldozer. It is incredibly stupid and shortsighted. There are areas of Norfolk and Suffolk which resemble the Canadian prairies. As far as the eye can see, one is confronted with a featureless landscape of cornfield, poisoned and polluted by pesticides. Because there are no hedgerows to contain the topsoil, much of it is blown into the North Sea and lost forever. Some English hedgerows are hundreds of years old, and once a hedgerow is ripped out, it can take generations to regrow - a conservationist once pointed out to me that 'every foot of an English hedgerow is a miniature national park'.

In Africa, there are so many controversial issues concerning conservation. Of one thing I am certain, that the only future for wildlife in Africa, or India, is that it must pay its way. There is no room now for the sentimental approach to wildlife. It is too late for that. Conservation must go much deeper. Africa's treasure must be a sustainable resource. It is certainly a renewable resource if only it is left alone. On countless occasions when I have spoken to audiences, and in particular children, in Zambia and other Third World countries, I have said that their wildlife is a treasure which few other countries have. It can be sold as a commercial commodity to all the wealthy tourists from the First World who will pay big money to go to countries in Africa to see wildlife, and the money will pay for the hospitals, schools and roads which Zambia and other countries need so badly.

I saw a marvellous example of this at first hand when we were making a film for Thames Television, just outside the Luangwa Valley National Park in Zambia, we visited a brand new clinic, fully staffed by a nurse and a doctor. just a few years previously, they had no medical facilities whatsoever in that particular village. The clinic had been paid for by money from eco tourism - the animals in the nearby national park had paid for the village clinic. The local people had realised that their wildlife was more valuable to them if left alone, rather than left to the poachers. I always say to them, 'Stop the poaching. Your poachers are stealing your most valuable asset'. In so many places in Africa, this message is finally getting through, so this is the hope for the future.

I have been out with the anti-poaching patrols. For many years, I have believed that these brave Africans have never had the recognition that they deserve from the outside world. After all, they face death at the hands of the poachers. A number have in fact been killed by poaching gangs. When I went out with the patrols in the Luangwa Valley, times were very bad. The administration of Zambia's Game Department had all but broken down, and the morale of the anti-poaching teams was at a very low ebb. There were just two patrols of fifteen men each at that time, walking out on foot to patrol an area the size of Wales. They were armed with just three rounds of ancient 303 ammunition each, facing gangs with AK47s. They were badly paid, if they were paid at all, and some had no tyres for their bicycles, if they had a bicycle. No doubt some were being bribed to go over to the side of the poachers and they could hardly be blamed; they could earn more money that way. Now, happily, things are vastly improved. The Game Department is well administered, as are the Zambia national parks, and there are some fine and dedicated people determined to stop the poaching and to encourage tourism.

I am happy to say that the Foundation that bears my name has played a small part in this. For example, through a good friend of ours, His Royal Highness, Prince Bernhard of the Netherlands, we obtained no fewer than 400 uniforms from the Norwegian Army. The equipment was sent out to Zambia and those who are fighting the war against the poachers now feel recognized. It was a very humbling experience when, on a visit to Zambia recently, we sailed up the Zambezi river. At regular intervals, we stopped and went ashore at the various remote and scattered game camps along the river. The African game scouts knew that we were coming and the sergeant and his men were lined up in their 'new' uniforms to welcome us. The sergeant made a moving speech in excellent English, thanking us for the support that we had given them, and then promptly asked for more help! That's Africa! It is, however, very rewarding to know that with so little effort, it is possible to help by bringing moral and physical support to these brave people.

With regard to the poaching of wildlife, one point is worth mentioning. The poacher is invariably an African or Indian living on the bread-line, trying to support a family from his primitive little plot of land. He does not understand the issues of conservation. I have been told that one small elephant tusk or rhino horn, when sold on the black market, can keep a poacher and his entire family for twelve months. They cannot therefore be blamed. The blame must rest firmly on the shoulders of the multi-millionaires living in Hong Kong and elsewhere who bribe the poacher to do their filthy work for them. 'These people, who I equate in terms of crime with the Mafia drug barons in Miami, will stop at nothing until the last

rhino, elephant or tiger is dead.

The plight of the rhino, the tiger, the mountain gorillas and so many other species is now desperate. I may not be an ecologist, but I firmly believe that the tiger in the wild could well be extinct within five years from the time I write. There are already more tigers in zoos than there are in the wild. When I was born in 1931, there were thought to be 80,000 tigers of all 8 subspecies. Since then, the Bali tiger has become extinct; the Siberian tiger is reckoned to number fewer than 400; and two tigers are dying at the hands of poachers every day. So that fact speaks for itself When I first went to Zambia in 1964, I saw 8 rhinos in one day in the Luangwa Valley National Park. At that time, Zambia's population of rhino were reckoned to number some 3,500. Today, there are none.

Concerning the African elephant, that gentle giant for which I have so much affection and to which I owe so much, it was estimated that in 1970, the population was in excess of 3,000,000. In just ten years from that date, two-thirds of those elephants had died at the hands of poachers and now, in the 1990s, African elephants throughout the whole of Africa number fewer than 600,000. The reason for this sudden decline in population is simple - money. Rhino horn is now five times the value of gold. In the medicine markets in the Far East, in Taiwan and China. A tiger skeleton is now worth US $30,000. If you have US $5,000 to spare, you can buy a plate of soup made from tiger penis. It is believed in China and Taiwan that if the products from endangered animals such as the rhino and tiger are consumed they can cure medical ailments. If one goes to a chemist's shop in Taipei, in Taiwan, with a headache, for example, you can see aspirin at one end of the counter and rhino horn at the other. The locals will go for the rhino horn. For Westerners, these ideas are hard to believe, but it is a question of educating the people of the East before it is too late.

Is it all really worth it? Is it too late now to repair the damage? The very fact that I am asked these questions with increasing frequency means, I hope, that perhaps more and more people are at last waking up to the realisation of what man has done to this fragile planet in the last seventy-five years or so. At the eleventh hour, perhaps we are now beginning to realise just how dangerous it is to tamper with nature, to assume that we can use this world to our own advantage at the expense of all other species. It is a very stupid philosophy. Nature will always win and we are playing a dangerous game indeed. We do not own the world. We share it with all the other species. They depend on us, as we do on them. If man continues to destroy three species every day of the year,

which he does, then ultimately he will destroy himself - of that there can be no doubt whatsoever. I suggest that conservation is therefore the most important issue of all, for we are talking about man's own survival.

I remember the title of a television programme shown many years ago - 'Through lack of interest, tomorrow has been cancelled'. We are only one minuscule part of the balance of nature which we have set out to wreck and destroy so catastrophically. If we do not learn this message now, it will be too late. To quote the words of the late and great Gerald Durrell 'We are destroying the world at the speed of an exocet, and we are riding on a bicycle'.

So, what of the future? Who can possibly tell, but we should worry very seriously about that future for the sake of our children and our grandchildren, for we are handing on to them what is left of this world.

While obviously we cannot predict the future in two, three or even four hundred years' time, there is hope because so many good things are happening. We know that Japan, the arch enemy of the whale for so many years, is still butchering 300 of these warm-blooded mammals in conditions of appalling cruelty every year, in the name of 'science'. What a nonsense! Are we really to believe they kill 300 whales a year for scientific research when it is, in fact, totally unnecessary? Whale research can be done benevolently. They are killing whales simply because there is a tiny minority of Japanese businessmen who will still pay large amounts of money to eat whale steaks in Tokyo restaurants. However, it is heartening to know that large numbers of young Japanese are now as sickened by the trade as are so many people in other countries around the world. I have learned recently of one Japanese whaler who claims to have killed more whales than anyone else - 6,000 from his factory ship. Now, he has found that he can make more money by taking tourists out 'whale watching'. The explosive harpoon on the front of his ship, which has caused so much suffering over so many years, has now been replaced by Japanese tourists armed with cameras. The motivation behind this change of heart may still be money, but the fact is that he is no longer killing whales.

Every two years, at some point in the world, the Convention on the International Trade in Endangered Species (CITES) meets to discuss the immediate problems of conservation and endangered species. A great deal of talking takes place and, at the end of the meeting, nobody is quite sure what has been achieved - certainly not enough. Nevertheless, it is heartwarming to know that a young Korean felt so ashamed of his country's record in conservation - one of the worst - that he decid-

With one of my friends

ed to camp in a tent, outside the recent CITES conference, for two weeks to protest at the fact that insufficient efforts were being made to save his country's wildlife.

The world seems to be ever more volatile and there are now more wars, albeit small ones, than ever before. It seems at times that we are hell bent on our own self-destruction through sheer stupidity. We seem to be growing up in an ever more money-grabbing society when finance is the only thing that matters. But all is not lost. I recently received a cheque for £1,800 from a 12 year-old girl who had decided to ride her bicycle with her mother across the widest part of the United Kingdom to help save the elephants that she loves so much. She is one of so many young people who show concern for the future and, with that in mind, I decided to ring up my local newspaper in the hope that they would write a story about this splendid young person. Such a story would, perhaps, go some way to redressing the balance, for we seem to read only of young people who are joy-riders and glue-sniffers. But not all young people are bad. It is my belief that they are the finest in the world of any generation, because they care about issues that concern our future. Sadly, the newspaper told me that they 'hadn't the space' to print the story. What a sad indictment it was of the age in which we live; wouldn't good news for a change make a welcome relief from all the stories of bad events we are overwhelmed with?

One of my deepest concerns is the almost complete indifference shown by so many heads of industry and people in power and influence who, if they really stopped to think about the future, could do so much more to help. They seem to be interested only in their shareholders and profit. I once wrote to the chairman of a large company who had big business interests in Taiwan. I suggested

that if he felt it appropriate and he had time, he could approach the Taiwanese authorities to bring to their attention the fact that they were the leaders in the extermination of endangered species. He wrote back as follows: 'While we share your concern for the plight of the rhino, the interests of our shareholders must come first'. What a stupid thing to say. He was expressing his almost unbelievable ignorance and total lack of awareness of public feeling. Did he not have the common sense to realise that many of his shareholders were undoubtedly conservationists and that, had they seen that letter to me, their first reaction would have been to sell their shares in his company?

I have recently read some chilling words in the glossy magazine of one of our major petroleum companies. The Writer an executive of the company, wrote an article about his parent company, Exxon, in the United States. He was extolling the virtues of what both were doing to help save the tiger to which they owe so much. Exxon is one of the biggest multi-national companies in the world and the largest petroleum company. They do not exactly have a clean record in conservation; I do my very best to ensure that no one will ever forget the Exxon Valdez disaster of some years ago. When that oil tanker was driven onto the rocks off the Alaskan coastline, the man in charge had been convicted previously of a drinkdriving offence. As if that fact were not bad enough, the tanker burst open and spread 54 million litres (12 million gallons) of oil along the Alaskan coastline. It not only did so much damage to the marine life in that area that the extent of it will never be known for certain, but it also caused the painful and slow death of 435,000 sea birds (that is the official number), and over 5,000 seals. I learn that Exxon have pledged US $255,000 (£175, 000) (to be spread over three years), for tiger research in Russia. Are we really to be grateful for that pitiful example of generosity?

I read further in the same glossy magazine words which left me with feelings of utter disbelief and stunned amazement:

Cold, windswept and wet, West Siberia holds few charms for any but petroleum geologists, whose studies in the 1930s identified it as a promising province. Serious exploration began in 1948... and by 1987, 350 fields and 1,000 reservoirs have been found. The northern half of the basin may contain the world's largest deposits of natural gas.

The article then went on to extol the virtues of this wonderful area which is full of potential, ready to be

exploited. Cold, windswept and wet, of interest only to petroleum geologists? What arrogance! I would suggest that that still unspoiled and wonderful wilderness is more than of great interest to the tigers and other wildlife species because they actually live in it! What it means is that yet another tiny unspoiled corner of an otherwise ruined planet is going to disappear forever, having been desecrated by man, in the interests of increasing profit. Two per cent of the world's land surface remains unspoilt, where wildlife, which shares this planet with us, remains undisturbed. It is their world too.

Do politicians really care? Some do, of course. Nevertheless as I write this, it is frightening to read that our own government is preparing to issue over fifty licences for gas and oil exploration around our coastline, many of which will affect environmentally sensitive areas. Our island is a very small one. Can we really afford to exploit it to this extent? We cannot.

During the interval of one of my many speaking engagements, when, happily, I seem to be able to raise a certain amount of awareness and really worthwhile sums of money for urgent conservation issues, a lady came up to me and asked, 'David, does it really matter if there are no more rhinos left in Africa? Give me an honest answer. I live in Wigan, and I am never going to be able to go to Africa to see them in the wild, because I cannot afford it'. I wanted her to listen. If I had just simply said that it does matter, she would probably have walked away. So, instead, I said 'No'. She was so surprised at this answer that I managed to hold her attention. I now took the opportunity to point out that, in the short term, the final extinction of rhinos in Africa would certainly not make the slightest difference to her daily life in Wigan. She would still be able to watch television in the evening and buy her cornflakes in the supermarket. However, in the long term, it did matter. Man, as I have already mentioned, destroys three species a day and if he continues on that path, he will destroy himself. I believe she got the message; at least she went away thinking about it. That is what matters.

We are destroying the rainforests of the world at the rate of 81ha (200 acres) every minute. In 1987, thousands of acres were burned in Amazonia and the fires of a single five - or six-month dry season released 620 million tonnes of carbon gases, a figure equal to about 10 per cent of all the pollutants in the world's atmosphere. Trees create the oxygen that we all breathe and on which we depend, and it is frightening to be told that in forty years' time, we will have virtually wiped out the entire rainforest belt of the world. This is not only a remarkable achievement, but is incredibly shortsighted, for we know that well over 40 per cent of the world's medicines come from plants. In those rainforests which we are destroying, there may well be precious sources of medicine from plants still unknown to science and which may be cures for heart disease, cancer and aids.

Through Man's unmatched ability and rapacious appetite to destroy everything around him, we have the potential to create catastrophes of awesome proportion through global warming. For example, we are capable of raising the levels of the oceans and this is already happening. I have read a report that states that within fifty years from the time of writing, we may well have drowned the entire country of Bangladesh. Where are those teeming millions going to go? There is certainly no room even to sit down in the next door country, India.

One man who has had more impact on my whole thinking on conservation than anyone else is Neil Armstrong. I met him at a party in Washington shortly after he had returned from the moon. It is not every day that one is lucky enough to meet someone who has walked on another planet and who, as a result of that momentous experience, has become a conservationist. I know, because he told me. I was determined to meet him, if only to tell my grandchildren that I had met someone who had 'walked on the moon'. I was finally introduced to him by my host, but not as a wildlife artist; he had no idea who I was. I was introduced to him as a conservationist and this word induced him to turn to me, when he said, 'David' I am a conservationist, too. You have to be, when you have been to the moon and back. ... As I was coming back from the moon, I looked through the window of my space capsule at planet earth, and seeing it brilliantly lit and floating all by itself in space looking very lonely, I suddenly realised when it was about the size of a golf ball [at this point, he raised his hand and joined his thumb to his first finger and formed a little circle] just how fragile it looked'. When a man who has stepped back at a distance of 402,000 km (250,000 miles) from planet earth and looked at it from space says it is fragile, it gives a whole new meaning to the word.

Children the world over are now beginning to realise just how fragile this planet is. I started a little experiment many years ago in Zambia when I asked some children 'Which is the most dangerous animal on earth?' At that time, they all gave me the wrong answers - elephants, lions, crocodiles and the rest. Now, whenever I ask children the same question, I always get the right answer - 'Man'! So the message is getting through.

Young people in Zimbabwe, for example, are protesting vociferously against the official philosophy that the tsetse fly should be exterminated. The tsetse fly is, in fact, the greatest friend that African wildlife has. Where there are tsetse flies, there are no cattle. For far too many years, the philosophy has been to exterminate the tsetse fly and introduce cattle. Tourists will not come to Zimbabwe to see cattle. They will come to see wildlife and the latter generates infinitely more foreign exchange than the former. It is as simple as that, but it is not always so easy to get the message across to those who make decisions.

Eco tourism is a vital ingredient in the conservation of wildlife in the countries that are fortunate enough to have such a priceless asset in their care, but it must be developed in a controlled way. The southern countries of Africa, such as Zambia, can learn so much from mistakes that, I believe, have been made in the north. There are many examples in East Africa where, through lack of control, mass tourism is in danger of all but destroying the environment and the very wildlife which tourists are paying to come to see. Someone once said to me: 'David, they have ruined the Kruger National Park. They have got tarmac roads and it is so artificial'. I pointed out that the very creation of a national park in the first instance is in itself artificial. Whatever its size, it is still a captive unfenced area, surrounded by habitation. When I first went to Amboseli, in the shadow of Mount Kilimanjaro in 1949, for example, we slept in tents. It is now one of the most popular places on the African continent. Vehicles are allowed to roam at will across the fragile topsoil, driving wherever they wish, creating dust storms. It is already an artificial situation and I believe that it can only be improved by building tarmac roads on which the vehicles are contained.

I have been told that the impact of mass tourism on one park in East Africa has had such an effect on cheetah that they have learned that they can only kill in the afternoon. If they are seen hunting in the morning, they are immediately chased by a string of mini buses crammed full of tourists with their cameras, in hot pursuit. How can any animal kill in those circumstances? The cheetah have learned that the tourists, after lunch in their lodges, go to sleep in the heat of the afternoon. That is when the cheetah are left alone.

Hunting must also play a part in the conservation of wildlife. I could not kill anything and it is not always easy to paint pictures of African wildlife for those who do. There is good and bad in every class of society; there is a good hunter and a bad hunter. I have met them both. Many years ago, I was asked to paint a Derby eland. I hardly knew what a Derby eland looked like. My potential client took a photograph out of his wallet to show me, hoping that I would be so enthused that I would rush home and paint a picture of the animal for him. The photograph showed a dead and bloody eland lying on the ground and the man's wife proudly displaying her rifle with her foot on the carcass. I am afraid that gentleman never received his painting.

A good hunter is also a conservationist. The animal he kills is probably old and would no doubt soon die anyway. He shoots the animal according to the strict conditions laid down by his licence, usually in the company of a professional safari hunter. The money should go, in theory anyway, straight into conservation. It is now the last minute for wildlife everywhere and one cannot afford to be sentimental.

A few years ago, a number of my friends suggested that I form my own wildlife conservation charity. Until then I had happily raised money for various international wildlife conservation societies. I can best quote His Royal Highness, Prince Bernhard of the Netherlands, who graciously accepted my invitation to write a few words in the brochure of the David Shepherd Conservation Foundation:

David Shepherd is in the unique position through his paintings to raise large sums of money for the conservation of wildlife and the habitat. It seems to me wholly appropriate, therefore, that he should have his own charitable Foundation to co-ordinate his charitable activities and exploit and maximize his potential. As founder president of the World Wildlife Fund, I give him my wholehearted support.

They were kind words from a very dear man.

The advantage of the Foundation is that it is small. We have just four full-time staff and I am certain that those people who support us feel that their money will be well spent on vital and urgent conservation projects. Some years ago, for example, we heard of a female black rhino, a rare subspecies, pining away in her miserable concrete cage in Lisbon Zoo in Portugal, having lost her mate. Shibula may not have lasted much longer when, with the financial help of our friends in South Africa, we raised sufficient funds to rescue her. She spent fourteen days with a vet on a container ship all the way to South Africa. Such was the interest generated by this project in South Africa that the Air Force decided to lift her, completely free of charge, in a C130 Hercules Transport and to take her into a national park on the borders of Namibia. After a few months, we were told that she had two mates and was putting on weight. A few months ago, as I write, we had the joyous news that she had produced a calf, now named 'Dundagoss', meaning 'we have achieved' in the local dialect. We have already shortened her name to the affectionate 'Dundi'. We have been told by the South African wildlife experts that this is actually a 'world first'. It is the first time that a black rhino from a zoo has been reintroduced into the wild, mated by a wild bull, then given birth to a healthy calf which she is successfully rearing. The latest news is that she has now had 3 calves.

My painting of the mountain gorillas of Rwanda, which appears in this book, has raised some £30,000. We have sent this money to the Karisoke Research Centre in Rwanda which, during the course of the war, had been vandalised. The brave African anti-poaching patrol team had used the Research Centre as a base and they had to flee for their lives. The appalling war has done irreparable damage to the whole beautiful area; some parts of the virgin forests where the gorillas live have been mined, and cattle are moving in to some parts. People are encroaching on the area for firewood and all these factors mean that the few remaining gorillas are under desperate threat. Nevertheless, in spite of the insatiability of the whole country which will last for years, the Africans have returned to their posts and the money we have sent them will be used to repair their accommodation which, in turn, will boost their morale and encourage them to realise that they are being supported from the outside world in their marvellous work to save their gorillas from extinction.

The African elephant is, of course, in the forefront of my thoughts and fund-raising activities. As I write, the international ban on the ivory trade continues, which has devalued the price of ivory, so there is not such an immediate incentive to the poacher. However, there is considerable pressure, particularly from Zimbabwe, South Africa and Namibia, to remove the ban. Those countries are telling the world that they have too many elephants. There are so many controversial issues here; many experts, for example, believe that many of the elephants that come over from Botswana into Zimbabwe are, in fact, being counted twice.

The whole matter of culling is a delicate issue and this controversy will rage for years. Are there really too many? It is obviously sad to see them destroying huge mature trees, pushing them over simply to eat a few branches and then moving on to another one. Everyone who has been to Africa has seen such devastation. However, elephants are known as nature's architects; they are changing the landscape rather than destroying it. When they knock a tree over, the grass grows up and the plains' game zebra, antelope and so on move in.

Nevertheless, remedial measures have to be taken if it is proved conclusively that there are too many elephants in one particular area. Many of us have seen the traumatic scenes of culling from helicopters when an entire family is wiped out, including the babies. I think these methods are totally unacceptable and, after listening to game wardens for years, I believe that nature should be allowed to repair the damage that we have done.

The Tsavo, national park is perhaps a good example of this. In the early 1970s there was a catastrophic drought and, with so little to eat, the elephant population plummeted. Elephants, in conditions such as these, actually adjust their birth rate according to what nature can provide. It was a sad sight to see so many dying but, when the numbers had been reduced through natural causes, the vegetation recovered, the rains came, and the elephants built up their numbers again to what is now a healthy balance. I would suggest that nature knows all the answers. It is when man interferes that the problems start.

Some African countries, as a result of the poaching operations that have plagued them for so long, have now built up piles of ivory and this in turn has created another dilemma. Some of these countries are desperately poor and the governments concerned have contended that the ivory should be sold on the so-called 'legal market', and the money put into conservation. First of all, I do not believe that it is possible to distinguish between legal and poached ivory and, in any case, I doubt very much if the money raised does actually go into conservation; it is 'lost' in the national exchequer. Now the trade in ivory has been opened up, the poachers are having a field day.

Good things are now happening in Zambia. In February 1992, in the face of strong opposition from her southern neighbours, the government was persuaded to burn her 8-tonne stock-pile of ivory and rhino horn, as a stand against the ivory trade. I have believed for many years that it is wrong for the First World to preach in an arrogant way to the Third World and tell them how to run their affairs. It would have been quite wrong if, having suggested that they burn all their ivory, it was left at that. £114,000 was pledged by the Foundation to the National Parks and Wildlife Service for their elephant conservation programme as compensation for the loss of any future income which they might have obtained from the sale of the ivory if the ban was lifted. I believe that this is the way to sort out such a problem and the elephant population in Zambia is now recovering. Elephants are not stupid. Those in Zimbabwe, for instance, know that if they stay there, they stand a good chance of being shot in the culling operations, so they are swimming across the Zambezi river into Zambia where they know they are safer. The poaching in Zambia is now very much reduced and the Zambian people are beginning to realise that their wildlife is worth more to them if it is left alive than if it is dead.

Man, through his infinite stupidity, has an unparalleled ability to destroy everything around him. Through his infinite wisdom, he has the ability to repair the damage, but he has very little time left in which to do so. The future of life on earth now is in the hands of our children. Time is running out fast for the tiger, the great whale, the tropical rainforests and countless species of bird, plant and insect, all of which form part of the intricate and priceless eco system of our natural environment.

I feel privileged that I have been one of those relatively few people who have experienced, and been a small part of, the great African scene which forever leaves such an indelible mark on one's mind. The early Victorians wrote of 'darkest Africa'. It is hard to imagine a more inappropriate description of a landscape that is a blaze of sunlight. To someone who has been there and whom the magic has touched, words from someone else are unnecessary; he already knows. Africa or India calls the traveller back time and time again. One can remember forever the smell of early morning in the bush when it is still cool; the sun rising; that sudden sunrise when it is immediately full daylight and life begins to stir; and how, at night, one feels totally at peace with nature under an African sky impossibly filled with stars. On foot, as I have been so often at Savuti, to find oneself just 3m (10ft) away from fifteen wild bull elephants, is a thrill beyond description. They trust me and I trust them.

Have I now been in on the final act? I cannot help but wonder. Is there really room on earth for the magnificent elephant or the prehistoric rhino? However tragic it may be when a beautiful man-made object such as a great painting 'is destroyed, it can always be recreated somehow. But when we have shot the last rhino or tiger, we can never recreate it, however clever we think we are.

I once heard these words: 'We have not inherited this world from our parents. We have borrowed it from our children and I hope to God that we have something worthwhile to hand on to them'. That is what conservation means.

Many years ago, someone was very complimentary when they said that, 'the best thing that ever happened to Africa's wildlife was when David Shepherd failed to be a game warden'. If the implication behind that statement was that I have managed to do more for the animals to which I owe all my success through my paintings than if I had been a game warden, then I am a very lucky and happy man.

MARCH SUNLIGHT

Although I painted this in the mid-1960s, I still regard it as one of my most satisfying landscapes. The original is in Johannesburg, and the painting certainly has an interesting history.

The print of *March Sunlight* marked my transition from unlimited prints into limited editions. The painting was published in 1967 and was the last of the mass-produced prints that appeared in their thousands in the chain stores and galleries throughout this country and abroad. A number of these paintings, *Wise Old Elephant*, *Winter Plough*, and others, had achieved enormous success and had helped to promote my name. However, with the success of *Wise Old Elephant*, for example, danger signals started flashing; I was getting the most appalling publicity as 'Britain's Top Pop Artist'. I realised that I

would have to be careful, otherwise my reputation could be endangered through becoming 'over-popular'.

It was with some anxiety that I learned *March Sunlight* had been judged the top selling print in 1967. This resulted in immediate and quite extraordinary publicity. The art critic of *The Evening Standard*, in his infinite wisdom, decided to write about the print under the heading 'Sex Symbols', which has led to the painting being known as 'My Sex Painting' ever since. You can read what he said in the text of this book!

As to the painting itself, in my diverse life I am fortunate enough to have been to the steaming jungles of Borneo, India and Malaya, the frozen wastes of northern Manitoba, the arid deserts of Arabia, and the sunlit landscapes of Africa. However,

it is always marvellous to come home, and there can never be a lovelier subject than an English landscape on a winter's day, when a watery sun casts long shadows from the elm trees across a ploughed field.

To me, the English elm, surely the loveliest of trees, epitomises such a scene. Sadly, in England mature elm trees are now a thing of the past, due to Dutch elm disease, and, for those who really look, the whole face of the English landscape has changed. When will we see the likes of these great trees again? With their winter tracery silhouetted against a cool, grey English winter sky and with rooks nesting in their upper branches, they create a picture that is surely one of the glories of the English countryside.

SHEPHERD STREET, MAYFAIR

During my years with Robin Goodwin, I must have painted nearly a dozen pictures in this part of London. We used to sell our pictures to the tourists, straight off the easel, unfinished and still wet. No one would pay me £25 for this one, so I kept it.

The Austin A40 dates the picture at 1955: the Magna Restaurant has been closed for many years and Shepherd's Pub (no relation) has been painted another colour, in my opinion, nothing like so attractive. The little dog actually did come along and lift his leg when I was working on the painting so he became part of the picture.

Nowadays, it would be impossible to set up an easel in such a place – with the crowds, pollution and traffic chaos. In any case, too many of the Victorian shop fronts have been replaced with plastic horrors, and ghastly high-rise blocks now dominate the skyline.

LUDGATE HILL IN 1890
(Reproduced by permission of W.N. Sharpe Ltd)

In the early part of my painting career, I painted some thirty pictures for Christmas cards and the company who printed them still own most of the originals. As far as I can remember, I was paid around £30 for each original painting, including the frame *and* the copyright, but I suppose that was quite a lot of money in those days!

They were very nice people to deal with; the hard part was having to flog my little car up the old A5 to Bradford (it was long before motorways) and back again in the evening. I was a lot younger in those days.

Ludgate Hill in 1890 was the most popular of all the subjects I painted for them and they have reproduced it many times in their Christmas card lists. A painting like this requires an enormous amount of research. If I had made any mistakes, either I or the Christmas card company would have been bombarded with phone calls with complaints such as: 'He's got the wrong train going over the bridge.' I didn't; I got the right one. 'Ready made two-piece suits did not cost 16/6d in those days.' They honestly did!

In fact, all the advertisements on the shop fronts and the buses are absolutely correct in every detail.

All the paintings I did for the company had to have snow in them; after all, they were going to be Christmas cards. I was usually asked to put a dog in as well. In those days I couldn't paint dogs; I am not sure that I can now. Of one thing I am certain, the breed of the animal in the picture is, to say the least, slightly obscure!

LIFE GOES ON – SEPTEMBER 1940

I was nine years old during the Battle of Britain and living in North London. Collecting bits of shrapnel and pieces of crashed German aircraft was of the greatest excitement for us small boys. Even having a load of incendiary bombs dropped in the field next door and rushing out before the police got there to collect the tails was fun! I don't think we realised that people were killing each other as we heard the rattle of machine guns and watched the twisting vapour trails in the blue sky above as we went to school.

As my record of the Battle of Britain I have resisted the temptation to paint the more obvious airborne battle scenes. I have tried to record the 'feel' of those momentous days as, in the true British spirit, life had to go on. I well remember such a picture as I have painted. In spite of the fighting overhead and aircraft crashing all around in the fields of Kent, Sussex and Surrey, the harvest had to be gathered in and nothing was going to interrupt it!

WINDSOR OAKS

Nineteen fifty-three was a gloriously hot summer. For many years I had been attracted by the marvellously gnarled and twisted shapes of the incredibly ancient oak trees in Windsor Great Park – some, I was told, having been mentioned in the Domesday Book. With the unpredictable English weather for once kind to me as day followed day of brilliant sunshine, I spent a week painting this particular tree which, it seemed, would be there for all time. A large chunk of the tree had broken away (probably in about the year 1400!) and it gave me a wonderful opportunity to indulge in my passion for painting dead wood – a passion which was to develop several years later, in Africa.

I feel that this painting 'came off' quite well and, like a few others of that period, I have kept it because no one would pay me the original asking price of, I think, £50.

ST PAUL'S FROM THE THAMES

Robin Goodwin and I painted a number of pictures from this vantage point on the Thames. As always, the conditions were hardly conducive to good painting. On one occasion, the wind caught his canvas, and, too late to catch it, he last saw it floating down the river and out to sea!

I wonder what Sir Christopher Wren would think now if he saw the changes we have made to the London skyline. He would probably turn in his grave. He designed his magnificent cathedral to be the central focus of the City of London. Now, when viewed from the opposite river bank, his magnificent edifice almost disappears when it is overshadowed by the faceless high-rise blocks of the Barbican Centre.

So much has changed since I worked on this painting. London's river is, of course, a great deal cleaner now and this must be a good thing. However, from my point of view as an artist, it is not quite the same. The old-fashioned steam tugs, bustling backwards and forwards with their long lines of barges, have been replaced by the modern diesel. This is more efficient, no doubt, but the atmosphere, for a painter, has all but disappeared, and to me it is atmosphere that counts. Although the mud is still there – lovely stuff to paint – it is no longer a 'smoky Thames'.

THE CURIO SHOP

This was one of the many delightful subjects that I painted, from life, in the area of Shepherd Market, London, in the late 1950s and early 1960s.

The subject attracted me because the little shop was crammed full to bursting with copper and brass pots and pans, all glinting in the sunlight. I painted three separate pictures of this subject from three different angles. The first one was purchased by the owner of the shop himself. He hung it inside, surrounded by all the antique bits and pieces; to the best of my knowledge, it hangs in the shop to this day.

THE BRABAZON HANGAR AT FILTON, BRISTOL

I had roof girders before my eyes for weeks after finishing this picture. I painted the whole thing 'from life'.

Although I received every possible co-operation from the lads in the factory, I did have a few problems. I was painting the airliner on the left when, suddenly, the hangar doors were opened and they started towing the aeroplane out.

'Leave it, please,' I called, 'You're ruining my painting.'

'Sorry, mate, we've got to deliver it to BOAC.'

They were super and so they pushed it back in again. 'BOAC can wait.'

The Bristol Aeroplane Company felt they couldn't afford £30 so I still have the painting. Forty years later I saw a gentleman looking at it and I asked him if he was interested in it. 'I should be, mate. I was one of the blokes who kept feeding you with cups of tea while you were painting it,' he replied.

BRITANNIA OVER KILIMANJARO

I painted this picture in the early 1960s and it was one of the first of my paintings to be published as an ordinary print.

I shall always remember my very first view of Africa's highest mountain, rearing skywards at a height of 5,800 metres (19,000ft). I was driving down to Amboseli from Nairobi with a friend and, suddenly, I realised that it was not a cloud that I was looking at on the horizon; it was the white snow-capped dome of Mount Kilimanjaro, shimmering in the heat haze as if hanging in space.

I have often wondered how many people have photographed Kilimanjaro. Little did I imagine when I painted this picture, that I would also come to portray my favourite mountain from a more conventional angle, with elephants in the foreground.

READING CATTLE MARKET

It's a long time ago now and I cannot really remember what inspired me to paint this scene. What I do know is that after I had finished my training I had plenty of time to choose my subjects, and a cattle market made a change from aeroplanes and steam trains. Furthermore, this highly paintable scene was not entirely unlike a steam locomotive shed. The sun cast beams of light through the cigarette smoke, and the back views of the marvellous characters sitting in the audience gave me plenty of material as they watched the hustle and bustle of the cattle auction; there was certainly plenty of atmosphere!

HIGHLAND CATTLE

The Victorian landscape painters of the nineteenth century seem to have had an obsession for painting threatening storm clouds swirling around the brooding mountain scenery of Scotland, crofters herding sheep along the stony mountain paths, and, it seemed inevitably, Highland cattle drinking at the water's edge. Undoubtedly, some of these great many paintings were more successful than others!

Travelling recently in the Highlands and coming round a corner on a remote mountain road I actually came face to face with these friendly and indeed, highly paintable, animals. I could now see why they appealed to my Victorian predecessors, and I hope that in my painting I, too, have managed to do justice to these marvellous wild and woolly animals, in the setting of surely some of the finest scenery in the world, of which they are so much a part.

CITY OF GERMISTON

Some years ago now, I promised my long-suffering wife that I would stop collecting 'large toys'. Avril has never once over the years said to me, 'Isn't it enough to buy *Black Prince*, *The Green Knight*, bring home an engine and a coach from Africa, and then set up a complete railway in Somerset?' She has never said it, but I am quite certain she has thought it.

I broke that promise a few years ago. I was being interviewed on South African television, on the Breakfast Show. My interviewer knew that I was 'potty' about steam engines, so he said, 'David, get in a plug about wanting a 15F – someone may

be listening.' Someone was. Shortly after the programme, South African Railways rang up the television studios: 'What's this about David Shepherd wanting a 15F?' That is when the project was born. It was agreed that if I painted a picture of one, they would give me a fully restored 15F Class locomotive.

It was a most marvellous ceremony. Three hundred people were on the platform at Kimberley Station. When I made my speech (difficult because I was getting excited), I knew what was going to happen. Behind me was 15F Class No 3052, fully restored and in a fresh gleaming coat of paint, with nine

coaches behind her. After my speech, she stormed into the station and the engine was handed over to me. We rode off down the line and had a lovely time. What a marvellous way of enjoying oneself!

The painting portrays a 15F Class, doing the job that it was designed to do, hauling freight trains, past one of the 'gold tips' around Johannesburg.

I fully intend to bring the locomotive home to England one day, but that's another story.

COMET OVER TOWER BRIDGE

I wonder how many other artists would be mad enough to paint London from the air. Every detail has to be correct; if there is even the smallest mistake, I would be bombarded with telephone calls from those who are determined to find fault.

This painting was on view in the window of a department store in Oxford Street, causing an enormous amount of interest to the passers-by. I quickly realised, as I was standing in the crowd listening to the comments, that there is no better way of getting a genuine appraisal of one's work than when those around you do not realise that you are the artist. One or two people were showing off their great knowledge of London by 'picking holes' in the painting. However, I had taken a great deal of trouble to ensure that the picture was accurate. When I reminded them that they did not know London as well as they thought, they were rather embarrassed, but were very nice about it.

My choice of aircraft in the painting, a Royal Air Force Transport Command Comet 4, was deliberate. I thought that if I included this most beautiful of airliners, in Royal Air Force colours, the Royal Air Force might purchase the painting. Happily, they did.

SLAVE ISLAND

It was an amazing experience to work in a boatyard that had hardly changed since biblical times. I was watched by the Arabs, who had never seen oil paint, or brushes, or a canvas before. They were fascinated as I squeezed the paint out of the tubes; they even asked if I was writing a letter home!

This painting changed my life. It was on the strength of it that the Royal Air Force in Aden offered me a trip down to Kenya with them. When I arrived in Nairobi, the Royal Air Force commissioned my very first wildlife painting; I could say that a very large part of my success emanates from this picture.

MUKALLA

In this modern age, it is a thrill for an artist to be able to visit a place that has hardly changed with the passage of time.

When I was in Aden in 1960, the Royal Air Force were determined to show me Shibam; getting there meant staying for a day or two in Mukalla. In those days, only eight Europeans lived there and a few battered motor vehicles drove around the town; otherwise the place was virtually cut off from the outside world except by the occasional flight into the airstrip, or by sea. There was certainly no hotel to stay in. I stayed with the political resident whose house, a lovely white-painted building on the sea front, had a Union Jack flying from the masthead; I felt very proud as the standard was hauled down by the Arab guard of honour every evening to the sound of the last post. To me, it represented just one small and fading relic of British influence in this part of Arabia.

SHIBAM

Shibam, built of mud bricks, has been called the 'Chicago of the East'. I feel sure that I must be one of the very few artists who has ever managed to visit this remote place. When I was there in 1960, it was virtually cut off from the outside world, no Europeans lived in it and there was no electricity. I managed to spend just a few hours in the town and was able to take some photographs from which I was able to paint this scene.

Now, I am told, a tarmac road runs all the way up there, and it has a video shop in the town centre. How lucky I am to have seen the place when I did.

EVENING AT THE WATERHOLE

I have a feeling that by now, the elephants of Savuti actually know me.

Savuti is probably the only place in Africa where it is possible to get out of one's vehicle and walk to within touching distance of these lovely gentle giants, as I have done. The bull elephants at Savuti have so far been relatively undisturbed by poachers and so are completely unafraid. They also know that in the dry season, this waterhole is the only source of the water that they so desperately need, so they come back year after year. The place provides me with wonderful material and it makes a particularly lovely subject in the evening light, with the impala, the doves, and my beloved 'Jumbos', not to mention a couple of warthogs thrown in for good measure.

THE LAND OF THE BAOBAB TREES

The Africans call it the 'upside-down tree'. They believe that when God went back to heaven, he had a few seeds left in his pocket which he casually discarded and they grew the wrong way up. Many examples that one can see of these magnificent and centuries-old trees certainly convey this impression.

Elephants love to chew the soft fibrous bark, possibly for its calcium content. Sadly, this often causes the tree to fall, sometimes with tragic results – elephants have been crushed by trees falling on them. These two great giants are very much part of the African scene.

ARNHEM BRIDGE, THE SECOND DAY

Anyone who goes to Arnhem cannot fail to feel the atmosphere in this town, the scene of one of the great, but tragic, battles of World War II.

If an artist paints for the Armed Forces, he has to be accurate in every detail. This means visiting the location. I made four trips to the town, and during these visits met many of the Dutch civilians who had lived through the horror of the battle during 1944. I could never have painted the picture had I not had their help.

We enlarged a photograph taken by a Royal Air Force Mosquito flying over the bridge at 5:00pm on the second day. This enabled me to record every detail of just one small part of the desperate battle fought by the Parachute Regiment to hold onto the all-important bridge, a fight that has now passed into the annals of military history.

CHECKPOINT AT FORKILL

This was one of two subjects commissioned by the Green Howards.

Forkill is an attractive little place surrounded by green hills, but, in the time of the 'troubles', it was also in the heart of republican 'bandit country'. So, although while I was walking around in sunshine, watching the little red van delivering the post, everything seemed to be completely normal, it was not.

I have never been trained as a soldier. I was walking with a foot patrol down a country lane and looking for vantage points from where I might be able to paint a suitable picture. I was just about to open a gate to go into a field when I was very forcibly shouted at by one of my soldier friends: 'Don't go through there, David. It could be booby-trapped.' It had never occurred to me.

The subject of the painting is actually the border between the Irish Republic and Northern Ireland where all cars and their occupants had to be checked. To me, an air of uncertainty always seems to be present at such a place. I felt very privileged to have experienced at first hand the day-to-day life of the British soldiers in that troubled part of the world, a day of boredom, mixed with tension.

CHRIST

Someone once came up to me and said, 'I thought you were dead, David.' This sort of comment is hardly a tremendous boost for one's morale on a Monday morning!

I know why they say these sorts of things. There is still, sadly, a popular fallacy that an artist is only likely to achieve success long after he is dead. Unfortunately, history has, to a degree, proved this to be the case. Poor old Van Gogh cut his ear off in desperation because he couldn't sell anything; now his pictures fetch millions and he doesn't benefit. I would far rather reap the benefit and see the possible enjoyment that some of my pictures might give to people while I am still alive. If, during my lifetime, I am becoming known to a few people, then I am flattered beyond belief.

If I do occasionally manage to diversify and paint subjects other than wildlife, the usual comment is, 'Oh, I thought you were the bloke who painted elephants.' I certainly owe an enormous degree of my success to my 'Jumbo' paintings. Nevertheless, if by some miracle I am remembered for any of my work after I have departed from this earth, I would dearly like it to be for my painting of Jesus Christ.

The painting hangs in the Army Garrison Church at Bordon and the military authority do their best to look after it. However, because this painting means more to me than any other, it does sadden me to realise that so few people see or even know of this picture.

Recently, there was an occasion during which more and more people were able to see the picture. My namesake, David Sheppard, the Right Reverend, the Bishop of Liverpool, and I did a joint fund-raising promotion in Liverpool Anglican Cathedral. I, like so many others, have visited many of the great cathedrals of this country, but, in my opinion, Liverpool Anglican Cathedral is one of the most glorious. It was a highly emotional moment to have my painting of Christ, all 6 x 2.5 metres (20 x 8ft) of it, hanging for just a few days in this great building – it looked so small, it was almost lost! However, it generated a tremendous amount of interest and I felt that for a short time, the painting was really being noticed and appreciated by more than just a few.

ON SHED – AS WE REMEMBER THEM IN THE LAST DAYS OF STEAM

In the cathedral atmosphere of the great steam sheds, engines 92203 and 75029 await their turn on duty.

Towards the end of Britain's great steam age in 1968, the locomotives were grimy workhorses, in the twilight of their years – neglected, forlorn, but still working. Here, in the gloomy depths of a round house, there was intense beauty of the most dramatic kind if you looked for it through the dirt and the grime. Shafts of sunlight penetrated broken panes of soot-caked glass in the roof, pierced through the steam and smoke, and played on pools of green oil on the floor. Lovely harmonies could be found in the cool greys, browns and mauves of the dirty engines; and on the connecting rods one could detect the occasional glimmer of light where wet, slowly dripping oil caught the sun.

All was almost quiet as the great steam engines rested, ready to go out on the road. Only the occasional wisp of steam eddied up into the darkness of the roof and there was a constant murmur of gentle sound as the engines simmered.

In fact, BR Standard 9F 2–10–0, No 92203, was one of the last steam locomotives to be built in Great Britain in 1959, at Swindon. The Standard 9 could indeed be termed the ultimate in British steam-locomotive design, and the class consisted of 251 engines. I purchased 92203 from Birkenhead in 1967. She had spent her short working life for British Rail on, first, the Somerset and Dorset before going north and, finally, working the massive iron-ore trains from Liverpool docks. She was eight years old when I purchased her for £3,000, with spares thrown in for good measure. I have now owned her for almost four times her working life on British Rail.

BR Standard 4, number 75029, was one of a class of 79 mixed-traffic locomotives and she was also built in Swindon, in 1954. She was last stabled at Wrexham, having worked on the Cambrian Coast line and I purchased her in November 1967 upon her withdrawal from British Rail.

I have named the two locomotives *Black Prince* and *The Green Knight* respectively.

GRANNY'S KITCHEN

Perhaps I was inspired by the television series, 'Upstairs, Downstairs'; anyway, I decided to build our own Victorian kitchen in my garage. I commissioned a professional set designer and she organised everything from an original kitchen range to the fruit. The whole outfit came down to our farmhouse in an enormous truck and the set was built overnight. She also engaged a lady who would play the part of the Victorian cook; my eldest grandchild, Emily, who also appears in my painting, *Biscuits* (see page 69), played the part of the little girl.

We dressed up both the characters in Victorian costume and when I had done a few preliminary sketches, I engaged a friend of mine, a professional photographer, to take the necessary photographs. We shut them all in the garage and 'let them get on with it'. Within minutes I heard roars of laughter, so there was obviously no problem on that score.

This was one of my most satisfying Victorian paintings as it offered so many opportunities – from the lovely colours of the fruit to all the 'Mrs Beeton' paraphernalia, heaped upon the old pine table. The crazy part of the whole project was that eighty per cent of the kitchen, which was only in the garage for twelve hours before it was all dismantled again, did not even appear in the painting. However, I think the picture worked quite well.

BISCUITS

I love painting the gracious Victorian age. In this picture, our third daughter, Melanie, dressed up in Victorian costume, sits beside the fireplace (based loosely on one of the rooms in our lovely old Elizabethan farmhouse). She is nursing her youngest daughter, Georgina, known in the family, and to all her friends, as Peanut. My portrait of Muffin, our little bearded collie, hangs on the wall above, just to the left of her head.

Our first grandchild, Emily, Peanut's sister, has an obsession for biscuits. So has Haggis, a dog of highly dubious ancestry that Melanie rescued from Battersea Dogs' Home. On the ground lies 'Red Teds'. He has been my beloved bear companion for more than sixty years.

TIGER FIRE

In 1971, the World Wildlife Fund, as it then was, decided to launch Project Tiger, an international effort to save these beautiful animals from the brink of extinction. At that time, there were just 1,800 tigers in India. I decided to help by painting my very first tiger.

I had never seen a wild tiger, so I flew out to India in the hopes of seeing one and failed; nearly all of them had been shot or exterminated through poisoning and trapping. I came back to England and went to Howletts, John Aspinall's Wildlife and Zoological Park in Kent, where John allowed me to go in with

Zarif; I had never been in with a tiger before, but I am a very trusting person. It was the most amazing experience and we got on incredibly well. I took a series of photographs of this tame and friendly animal from which I did the painting. The limited edition print run raised a very worthwhile sum to help save the tiger.

As a result of Project Tiger, the numbers of tigers in the wild gradually built up, but now, sadly, they have crashed dramatically once again. This is due to the enormous value of tiger bones for medicinal purposes in the markets of Taiwan and

China. There are estimated to be only three thousand tigers left in the wild and they are disappearing fast.

I feel their loss passionately because, since painting *Tiger Fire*, I have been to Ranthambhore National Park and seen tigers in the wild. This has convinced me more than ever that they are the most glorious of all the cats. They deserve a better fate than they are facing at the moment, on the very edge of extinction.

BURNING BRIGHT

It's high noon in the Indian jungle. Only the monotonous droning and buzzing of insects disturbs the silence, in the cool, dark depths of the forest. Suddenly a Langur monkey shrieks and then the staccato bark of a Chital stag is heard somewhere in the distance. Could it be a tiger – that most glorious of animals?

Nerves tingle and the tension is almost unbearable as ears and eyes strain to catch even the slightest sound and move-

ment. Then, with scarcely a sound, as if a ghost, the King of the Jungle steps from the deep undergrowth, dappled into a mosaic of shimmering sunlight, forward into the cool water to slake his thirst.

In the Ranthambhore National Park, near Jaipur, I have seen and experienced such a thrill – the memory of which I shall treasure for always.

THE WIDE OPEN SPACES

I don't believe any photograph or painting can really convey the spirit of freedom and the wide open spaces of Africa in all their vastness. Standing under a huge, towering, thunder sky, looking into the limitless distance, I have felt very small indeed. The feeling is almost overpowering; even man himself, in spite of all his arrogance and apparent supremacy, is cut down to size; he is just a minuscule part of the overall scheme of things.

A long time ago, the African wild dog, the Cape hunting dog, was relatively common, but now, tragically, it has disappeared from so many parts of Africa and is now an endangered species. These marvellous animals have a quite unjustified reputation for being ruthless killers. In fact, they are marvellous to watch and have very strong family units; it is a joy to see them playing and looking after their pups. They, like all other species, play a very important part in the overall balance of nature which man, the most dangerous animal on earth, has done so much to upset. Long may these fascinating animals survive in the wide open spaces that they share with all of us.

THE ROADMENDER'S DAUGHTER

We were in Assam, driving along a very dusty track miles from the nearest civilisation, essentially looking for tigers, when suddenly we came across a primitive bridge being rebuilt by the ladies of the village, who were humping great rocks around on their heads. (All the men of the village were asleep under a tree.) As we drove past, I noticed that there were a number of small children, dressed up as though they were going to a party, sitting in little wicker baskets, which in turn were tied to trees. I never discovered why.

It is always so easy to miss wonderful subjects for a painting.

It must have been five miles further on up the road before the compulsion to take photographs of the children was so strong that we had to turn back. The result was this painting.

BUFFALO WALLOWS

There is a place in the Tsavo East National Park in Kenya called Buffalo Wallows. Covering many square miles of parched and dry red landscape near the Galana river, it is a landscape of huge rocks, jumbled together in chaotic profusion, interspersed with dry gullies. Here, around a corner, one can quite easily be suddenly confronted by either an elephant or a buffalo, of which there are many in the area.

This wild landscape seemed to be an ideal setting in which to portray the African buffalo. I have seen countless numbers of these magnificent animals over the years and I never fail to be inspired by them and that moment of tension as I suddenly see a group of them standing gazing at me, their noses sniffing the air and their eyes peering intently at the intruder.

SERVICE BY NIGHT

King's Cross Station in 1955; it is very different now. Apart from everything else, the signal box has been demolished and the steam trains have gone. It is all very clinical and nothing like so interesting.

It was in the days of steam that I painted this picture, and sketching and taking photographs was quite a dangerous business. I had to be escorted out to the point in front of the tunnel mouth just outside the station because I could very likely have stepped over a line and got myself killed by a steam train coming out of the tunnel behind me.

I was excited beyond measure when British Rail Eastern Region bought the painting, including the copyright, for £60; they wanted to make a poster of it to put up on stations all over the country. However, for this it had to be correct, and it was full of mistakes. I didn't know anything about signalling or which train would come out of which platform – I had one train coming out of the milk yard, so that had to go.

When the painting had been passed in every detail, it went to print. All the copies had been produced when another major mistake, right in the foreground, was noticed. I had managed to get the points wrong which meant the train coming out of the picture would have promptly derailed. A poor man at the printers had to alter every single copy by hand. He can't have been very pleased.

NINE ELMS, THE LAST HOURS

In the half-demolished shed, it's the end of the line for 73155 and she stands forlorn and rusting. Merchant Navy 35030 is in steam for the last time – she has just run the final steam train into Waterloo and together, chalked with corny but sincere slogans of affection, they await their last journey, hauled by diesel to the breaker's yard and the cutter's torch.

Inspection pits are filling with ashes from fires now cold; old buckets, rubbish and twisted firing irons are everywhere – all the squalid impedimenta that mark the end of an era.

Nine Elms is still a 'wasteland', but of modern concrete now in the form of the new Covent Garden Market. What a tourist attraction it would be, had it been left exactly as it was on 7 July 1967.

THE OLD FORGE

With his dog always with him, his inseparable companion, the village farrier had arrived for another hard day's work.

This old forge was a marvellous subject for a painting. It was all there waiting – the ringing tones of hammer on anvil, the characteristic smell of singed hair as a new shoe is tried and fitted in clouds of smoke, and the light of the fire dancing among the cobwebbed beams of the ancient roof.

LAZY HAZY DAYS OF SUMMER

I love to recall the days of my childhood in the 1930s when life seemed to go by at a much more leisurely pace. The sun always seemed to shine in those days, bees buzzed in the hedgerows and the meadows were full of wild flowers and butterflies.

The tranquillity of this riverside scene, with the Shire mare and her foal dozing lazily, recalls for me memories of nearly sixty years ago. There were fewer cars and tractors then, and pesticides and pollution had not spread death and destruction throughout the countryside.

THE LUNCH BREAK

After a hard morning's toil loading up the harvest, both farm workers and horses pause for a well deserved break. This is the time to bring out the freshly baked bread, the cheese and the local brew.

My painting is set in the 1920s. This was an age of few cars,

and there was nothing to shatter the summer tranquillity. Against the backcloth of noble English elms, the sound of bees buzzing in the poppies and larks singing their song far above in the blue sky provided that timeless magic of a true summer's day in England.

The pace of life may have been slower, but for the workers on the farm, life was not that easy. I was told that the machinery on the farm was deliberately left unoiled because then the boss could hear the wheels squeaking and he knew his men were working!

81

PLAYTIME

How much less attractive this painting would have been had I painted my subjects in T-shirts and jeans. I had been to a theatrical costumier's to hire the outfits and there I saw rows of teddy bears sitting on the shelf. I knew that I had to be very careful in a painting such as this to get the details right – even the design of teddy bears changes over the years. One rather special bear was over eighty years old. The lady in the costumier's said, 'He doesn't go out very often because he is getting on a bit. However, if you look after him, we are sure that he would love a weekend in the country.' He was mine for the weekend and, on returning the clothes and the teddy to the shop, I was asked, 'Has teddy enjoyed his weekend? We do hope so.' Painting subjects like this is so enjoyable and I meet such nice people.

MUFFIN'S PUPS

In her first litter, Muffin, our bearded collie, produced eight glorious puppies. They all very quickly began to develop their own special and diverse characters. At the time I painted this picture, they were seven weeks old and getting to the point where the mayhem and pandemonium at feeding time was such that they were not only a burden to their mother, but to everyone else concerned. Also, perhaps, they were at their most irresistible. Tears flowed when the day came that they all had to be taken away to their new homes.

Muffin was a beloved member of the Shepherd family for thirteen years. She passed away on 6 June 1994. We have lost a dog of absolutely unique character and a true and devoted friend. Only those who have known such a loss will understand the hurt.

BLACK FIVE COUNTRY

Once in a while, man creates a masterpiece: it may be a great cathedral, or a symphony, or a painting. He can also create a classic machine – that rare achievement when not only our functional requirements are more than adequately met, but they are incorporated into a superlative design. Devotees of the steam locomotive have very strong ideas, indeed some might say fanatical. However, many would surely agree that in the 1930s William Stanier, of the London Midland and Scottish Railway, created a classic steam locomotive. His 'Black Five'

first came into service in 1934. No fewer than 842 examples were built, the last emerging from works in 1951.

I have often been criticised for painting 'sad' railway pictures. However, this scene at Stoke-on-Trent Motive Power Depot in the very last few weeks of steam is how many of us remember it. Our proud steam heritage did not go out in a blaze of glory as it should have done. Locomotives were in appalling external condition, completely anonymous under layers of filth. The ground was inches deep in grimy oil and ashes –

lovely stuff to paint! Sad it is, but that is how it was and that is the very stuff of nostalgia.

If the scene had been left exactly as I have portrayed it I suggest it might now be an enormous tourist attraction to which people would come from all over the world. It has all been cleared away and the site is now a mega-store and a housing estate.

OVER THE FORTH

It was a memorable experience to drive across this magnificent bridge in the cab of a locomotive many years ago. It reminded me strongly of going down the aisle of a great cathedral as the intricate tracery of the girders passed over me.

This great monument to late Victorian engineering took 5,000 men 7 years to build, and it consists of 148 acres of steel-work, taking 17 tons of paint every time it is painted. I asked British Rail how many rivets were used – the estimate was 6,500,000, or 4,200 tons. The last one was placed in position by HRH Prince of Wales in March 1890 and the bridge is still in fine fettle.

WINTER OF '43, SOMEWHERE IN ENGLAND

I owe an enormous debt of gratitude to the Royal Air Force because they commissioned my very first wildlife painting which changed the course of my life. How could I refuse, therefore, when the Royal Air Force Benevolent Fund asked me to raise money for them?

I had two exciting hours flying in the Lancaster that belongs to the Royal Air Force Battle of Britain Memorial Flight, and which is one of two that remain in flying condition in the whole world, out of seven thousand built. There was a Spitfire on one side and a Hurricane on the other, and I was as excited as any small boy could possibly be.

I hope that I have captured the memories and feelings which must still be fresh in the minds of thousands of ground crew and air crew, now dispersed all over the world, who worked on and flew their beloved 'Lancs' with the Royal Air Force during those momentous days of World War II. How many must still remember 'their' Lanc at a far-flung dispersal? I have tried to convey the feeling of a watery sun casting long shadows on a chill autumn evening, the leafless elms of a countryside 'somewhere in England'. Those who were part of these memorable scenes will remember the wet runway, the mud, and all the untidy clutter of the last-minute preparations before take-off. They will remember those final adjustments to an engine: 'The revs were a bit low on the port inner last night over Essen, Fred. It's Cologne tonight, so get 'em right,' and the inevitable bicycles. I hope it is all there – that sense of historic times.

I still own this painting because it means so much to me – not only did it raise a very large amount of money for the Royal Air Force Benevolent Fund, but I made so many friends while painting it. So I feel that in some small measure, I have managed to repay the enormous debt of gratitude I owe to the Royal Air Force. The limited edition prints of this picture raised £96,000 for the RAFBF.

ZEBRAS AND COLONY WEAVERS

The Etosha National Park in south-west Africa is more inaccessible than most other national parks and has an individual beauty all its own. A remote, harsh, dry and dusty landscape of rock and glistening white salt pans, even the sky is a different hue of blue. The waterholes team with wildlife. Etosha park also has some of the largest concentrations of zebra and gemsbok to be seen anywhere in Africa.

Amongst the most interesting features of the park are the huge nests built in the acacia trees by the colony of sociable weavers. These attractive yellow birds live in many hundreds in the huge masses of twigs and grass knotted together in the branches of the trees and which are their nests. Some of these communal 'cities' measure 4 metres (12ft) and more across, and can be 1.5 metres (5ft) thick. Many have been built up over a period of thirty years or more, attaining such a size that the host tree eventually collapses under their weight. This is my favourite sort of country, and Etosha and places like it call me back again and again.

THE WELCOME STORM

Towering and dramatic skyscapes are so much a part of the vastness of Africa. With a hush of expectancy, the parched land is awaiting the coming of a new season's rain. The grass has been scarce for many months since the last rain fell, and the wildlife is thirsty and restless; but the days of endless blue sky and searing sun are gradually giving way to threatening thunder clouds. Soon, the heavens will open and the landscape will be born anew.

The scene is the Luangwa Valley in Zambia, one of the finest national parks in the world and one of the last strongholds of the African elephant.

A GREATER KUDU

How can I possibly say, when asked, which is my favourite animal? (Apart from elephants, of course!)

It is a thrilling experience, indeed, to come across a group of greater kudu, the females with their calves, and, as head of the herd, a magnificent bull standing majestically looking at you, his huge horns curving up into the sky.

AFRICAN AFTERNOON

It is a sobering thought to realise that over one million acres of tropical rainforests could have been destroyed in the time that it has taken to paint this picture.

Of all the examples of man's ability to destroy everything around him, perhaps one of the most dramatic and significant is the issue of the annihilation of the rain forests being done in the name of money, corruption and greed. This destruction is very short-sighted and stupid. After all, it is the trees of the world that create the oxygen that we all breathe. They also sustain the top soil; cut the forests down, and the results are catastrophic floods.

I am reminded by the experts that 46 per cent of the world's medicines come from plants. Is it not possible, therefore, that in the rainforests of South America, there may be a plant species, as yet unknown to science, that could be the answer to our continuous and expensive search for a cure for the diseases that are still afflicting us? It is something for us to think about.

As a subject for my painting, I chose the beautiful bongo, a secretive antelope that lives in isolated pockets of deep African forest. This lovely animal seemed to me to represent those countless species that will disappear forever if the progressive destruction of the rainforests of the world continues at such a frightening pace. It is their world too. This painting raised £80,000 for the tropical rainforest campaign.

THE *ARK*, TURNING INTO WIND

I was commissioned to paint HMS *Ark Royal*, the last one, by the Fleet Air Arm Museum at Yeovilton. Of course, I had to see 'the *Ark*' for myself – I love playing with 'big toys'.

The Royal Navy flew me out to Malta where I joined the great ship on her last journey home to the scrapyard. Those eight days on board were among the most exciting in my life. The flight deck of a great aircraft carrier at sea is a hive of activity and if the Royal Navy had not looked after me so well, I think I would probably have got myself killed in all the excitement. Gannet aircraft were being towed with their wings folded, looking like huge birds, Buccaneers and Phantoms were coming up from the inner depths of the ship on lifts and then taxiing to the catapult for take-off. I had to wear protective equipment over my ears. The sight and sound of a twenty-ton

Buccaneer or Phantom with its Twin Spey engines at full throttle is beyond belief. At that point, generating as much power as a destroyer, the aircraft rears up like a prehistoric monster and strains for release from the catapult. It then accelerates from a standstill to 210 kilometres (130 miles) an hour in a couple of seconds. It was almost too much to bear.

I wanted to see the *Ark Royal* from the air so I spent most of the time in the air-sea rescue Wessex helicopter, an essential part of the operations when aircraft are catapulting off the deck. Through the communications system of the helicopter, I was able to talk to the captain and I found that asking him to just alter course by a few degrees to port or starboard changed the shadows and gave me new ideas for the picture. On the last day, I was getting rather carried away by all this. By now, I

was on Christian name terms with the captain and I said, 'Ted, do you think you could turn completely around and go back to Malta, because the sun is in the wrong position?' You cannot imagine the thrill and feeling of power that it gives a little boy like me when, a few minutes later, he sees 56,000 tons of Her Majesty's aircraft carrier turning around and going in the opposite direction.

Royal Navy hospitality was unsurpassed, except for the ghastly tea that was brought to me and poured out of a bucket at 5 o'clock in the morning. However, the print edition of the painting raised a really worthwhile sum for the Fleet Air Arm Museum, and was perhaps a just reward for providing me with one of the great thrills of my life.

WESTMINSTER '66

In 1994 it was a particular joy to paint this picture as it meant returning to my earliest days, when I so often painted such scenes of the city.

London's red double-decker buses are surely as much a part of our national life as Big Ben. The RT Double-Decker, the bus in the background of my painting, is regarded by many as being the most successful bus of all time, having been built in huge numbers. However, it was succeeded by the ever-popular and famous Routemaster. These were built in their hundreds with the idea that they would last ten years. Nearly half a century later, many are still running in London and elsewhere.

In 1994 I asked the Friends of the London Transport Museum if I could have a bus, for the David Shepherd Conservation Foundation, as a promotional vehicle. They agreed that an exchange could be arranged – a bus in return for a painting. *Westminster '66* now hangs in the London Transport Museum in Covent Garden. Meanwhile, a beautifully restored Routemaster in Greenline colours is busy being driven by a supporter of the Foundation all over the United Kingdom, promoting the cause of the tiger, the rhino, and other endangered species.

AVRIL

I have only painted half-a-dozen portraits, and they are all people who have played an important part in my life, as my readers will discover from this book. Of these portraits, two are of my long-suffering wife, Avril. The first one is in the cupboard under the stairs and no one sees it because I painted her when she had mumps. I suppose I was a bit naughty, dragging her out of bed and making her sit, but it was the only opportunity when we both had the time to spare. I painted her entirely from life and it is exactly like her, mumps and all!

This, the second portrait, was painted many years later when neither she nor I had the time to have her sit for me so I worked from photographs; the result is a more appropriate painting and perhaps more complimentary. Nevertheless, the artist knows that there is no better way than painting from life, so the first portrait has, to me, that extra, indefinable quality; but I will never show it to anybody.

DREAMING

I love the gracious clothes of the Victorian era and Mandy,
daughter, does too. She decided to go down to the lake to
the ducks. In the heat of a drowsy afternoon, she was r
away with her thoughts.

PORKERS

Piglets seemed to be running around everywhere. There were hundreds of them, from many different litters, grubbing around and playing in a field in the warm spring sunshine. I actually managed to capture five of these little characters from the crowd and I put them in a box and waited to see what would happen. Their immediate attempts to escape from their temporary confinement resulted in some splendid piggy expressions. Nearby, their mothers were grunting in blissful contentment as they wallowed in a cool mud bath.

In an increasingly commercial age, the need to make a quick profit seems to influence so many of our activities and inevitably results in such horrors as factory farming. So many people are now expressing their feelings of revulsion by protesting against the cruel confinement, in inhumane conditions, experienced by so many domestic animals being reared for meat. With all this in mind, what a joy it is to see, hopefully in increasing numbers, farmers who allow their pigs to run free in the fresh air, their natural environment. Perhaps things are changing for the better.

DONKEY TALK

For centuries the donkey, as a beast of burden, has been the most faithful, but in too many instances the most exploited of animals by man. We all know of the many cases of cruelty that have occurred through ignorance, particularly in Middle Eastern countries, so it is all the more gratifying when they are seen well cared for and with their young, as here on a farm near Fareham, in the south of England.

COTTAGE COMPANIONS

I have turned once again to the early Victorian past, an era of dimly lit inglenook fireplaces in smoky cottages.

Barbara posed for this picture with Muffin, our bearded collie. While Barbara was trying to get on with the spinning, Muffin was trying to persuade her that going for a walk would prove far more fun for the both of them.

The fireplace in my painting is in our own home, an Elizabethan farmhouse dating from 1560. In those days so long ago, the family would quite possibly sit inside the fireplace and draw a curtain right across for warmth. The original hooks to hold the curtain back are still in the brickwork and when I was preparing the fireplace for my picture, hanging the small curtain inside the old oak beam, I found some of the material of the original curtain still in place.

MR THOMAS AND MAJOR RICHARD LEVESON GOWER

A commission such as this comes once in an artist's lifetime. Mr Thomas and Major Richard lived on their own in a beautiful home full of valuable paintings and antiques and I was commissioned to paint their portraits, life-size, on a 2.5 x 4.3m (8 x 14ft) canvas. These were to hang in the fascinating house when, eventually, it was to be opened to the public.

I was honoured to have the painting accepted by The Royal Society of Portrait Painters annual exhibition in London and the picture drew a remarkable amount of interest. One feature which caused a lot of comment were Major Richard's lovely leather shoes; I heard someone say, 'They don't make shoes like that any more.' They also noticed that he had one blue and one brown sock!

WHILE THE SUN SHINES

The harvest is almost gathered in. A few stooks are yet to be loaded into the wagons and the horses are patiently waiting as the storm clouds gather.

I have turned the clock back once again to a more leisurely age when horsepower prevailed and the only sounds to be heard in the fields were the jingle of harness and bees buzzing in the sultry air of high summer.

THE MASAI

Until we came on the scene, these proud and independent people had been living in Masai land, on the borders of Kenya and Tanzania, for centuries. They have been determined in many respects not to have their traditional lifestyle influenced by the progress and development taking place all around them. Even so, changes have inevitably occurred.

When I first went to Amboseli in 1950, they ran at the sight of a camera. Now, in order to do this particular painting, I had to meet the chief first for long discussions about what I was allowed to photograph for the money that I was prepared to pay. It was strictly according to 'trade union rules'. For £10, I was allowed two warriors for one hour only, and the money had to be 'up front'.

To someone like myself who has been privileged to see Africa just a little wilder, this situation seems very sad, but I suppose it is inevitable. So many wealthy American tourists going to Amboseli have, over the years, thrown dollar bills around the Masai like confetti, simply to take photographs back to the United States. Money is the root of so many problems and it certainly has had an influence on so many of these fine people. On one occasion, my wife and I were filling up with petrol at the filling station at the gates of Amboseli National Park and two warriors, in their magnificent red-ochre clothing, were standing by the petrol pumps with their spears. One asked me, in perfect English, if I would like to take a photograph of him standing beside my wife. I declined and the prompt reply came, 'Don't you get on with your wife?'

In spite of all that I have said, a lot remains unchanged in Masai land. They still herd their cattle, running alongside the game with which they have lived in harmony for so long. Nevertheless, they are under continuous pressure or temptation to change.

I was told of a wealthy tourist who walked into a Masai *boma* (the traditional collection of mud huts) and approached the chief. 'Don't you miss not having a washing machine, a television set and a telephone?' I never heard the answer our tourist friend received from the chief, but I can imagine it. Who are to be envied? Is it the Masai with their lifestyle, or us with ours?

THE BUNGLE BUNGLES

I had never been to Australia before, but in 1992, I went to Perth with my Conservation Foundation to raise money for wildlife projects in Australia.

We had arranged to have an auction of various items and I naturally wanted to paint an Australian landscape because I felt that would be appropriate. Someone said that the Bungle Bungles would make a good subject – I had no idea what on earth they were talking about (it sounded rather like the feeling one might get having flown economy class from England to Australia!)

The Bungle Bungles are a most interesting collection of strange-shaped mountains in a remote area of north-western Australia, 'in the direction of Darwin'. I knew what that involved – distance means nothing in Australia.

Through the generosity of someone who had his own aeroplane we flew for seemingly endless hours, and, finally, landed on the most beautiful farm miles from anywhere, where we stayed the night. It was exactly as I had imagined. I asked the owner's wife where she did her shopping. 'We go up the road to Darwin,' was the reply. 'Up the road' was 300 kilometres (170 miles) away!

At first light the next morning, two Bell Jet Ranger helicopters, generously loaned by a local company, landed on the farm and we took off and flew for a long time over country that looked rather like Zambia; I almost imagined I could see elephant and rhino below. Then, in the distance, there appeared what looked like a series of huge red sandstone beehives towering into the sky in the beautiful early morning light; we had arrived at the Bungle Bungles.

We landed beside a dried-up river and although it was only 7:30 in the morning, the heat was already almost unbearable. To me, it was all so new and exciting that I started dashing around, pointing my camera in every direction. A hundred paintings were unfolding in front of my eyes.

I felt very happy with the result of my first Australian landscape. It raised a very worthwhile sum at the auction and the gentleman who bought it lives in London where it now hangs.

FEVER TREES

What can I, or anyone else, say about Amboseli, with its glorious backdrop of Mount Kilimanjaro, that has not already been said? I have painted this scene so many times and all I can say is that this particular one, I feel, is one of my better pictures and portrays my beloved elephants against the most perfect setting imaginable.

FIRST LIGHT AT SAVUTI

Savuti, in Botswana, to where I return again and again, is 'wild Africa'; there is none of the impact of mass tourism here.

The pride has been active during the night; they have eaten well and they will not kill again for some days. It has been a cold night and they are awake. Now, it is the dawn of another day. Dawn in Africa is a time of indefinable magic that those of us who have been lucky enough to experience can never forget. The first rays of light from an early morning sun bring fresh life into the landscape, lighting it up with brilliant colours, so soon to fade as the sun rises into the sky and everything slows down with the overpowering heat of midday. The lions themselves are feeling the first warmth of the early morning sun and soon they will slumber.

THE LOOK OUT

To see cheetah in the wild is an exciting experience when one considers how elusive they are. They have been much persecuted over the years as 'cattle killers', and are still regarded as vermin in parts of Africa.

Their very lifestyle has been affected and influenced by tourism. I have been told that in certain parts of East Africa, in areas of mass package tours, the cheetah only hunts in the afternoon. The reason for this extraordinary turn of events is a simple one. If a cheetah tries to hunt its prey in the morning, it will immediately be seen and chased by half a dozen buses filled with tourists filming the poor animal. Apparently, the cheetah now waits until the tourists have a sleep in the heat of the afternoon, knowing that this is its only chance to hunt undisturbed.

I remember a time when things were different; some years ago, I was driving with the game warden in the Serengeti National Park and it had been raining for hours. The windscreen wipers had ceased to function on the Land Rover and the front was covered in mud. We decided to stop to clean the windscreen and before we realised what was happening, a cheetah jumped onto the front of the vehicle. He obviously regarded this as a convenient vantage point from which he could see into the distance. The warden, obviously quite used to such an event, wound the window down and, to my amazement, put his arm out, got hold of the cheetah's tail, and started cleaning the windscreen with it. I have wondered to this day whether the cheetah ever realised that his tail was being used in such an undignified way; if he did, he didn't seem to mind.

SNOW LEOPARD

The snow leopard is now one of the world's rarest animals. This beautiful cat, so elusive and shy, lives its lonely existence in the remote high mountain regions of Nepal. It has been hunted mercilessly, almost to extinction, and is now rarely seen in the wild. Its fur is of a uniquely deep and soft quality and has remarkable variations of subtle colours, from cool grey to a warmer hue. Even now in the eleventh hour, its fur can still be obtained from the less reputable traders in India, Pakistan and even Greece and other European countries. As long as this trade is allowed to go on, this glorious animal will continue to decline in numbers.

ZAMBEZI SAWMILLS RAILWAY

It was in 1971, after completing a film on this amazing and antiquated Zambezi Sawmills Railway for BBC television, that I asked the President of Zambia, Dr Kenneth Kaunda, if I could have one of the old locomotives in the graveyard. He not only said 'yes', but arranged for me to have a coach as well!

The homecoming of the two vehicles over the Victoria Falls railway bridge, in the middle of sanctions, out through Beira in Mozambique, around the Cape, up the west coast of Africa, into Manchester docks, and down the M1 motorway, is quite a story in itself. This ancient locomotive, very nearly a hundred years old, spent seventy-eight years of its life working faithfully in Africa and has now returned home, to the East Somerset Railway.

THE PANDAS OF WOLONG

For many people considering the desperate plight of so many endangered species, the panda inevitably comes to mind; indeed this fascinating animal has been the very symbol of wildlife conservation for many years now.

Even today, little is known about the giant panda. What is certain is the fact that along with the tiger, gorilla, rhino, and so many other endangered animals, it is on the brink of extinc-

tion in the wild. So much is stacked against the chances of its survival, but it is primarily man's rapacious appetite for the exploitation of its natural habitat that is the panda's greatest threat. The future is bleak indeed. Nevertheless, efforts are being made and the Wolong Natural Reserve in Sichuan Province is the subject of my painting. This is an area of 2,000 square kilometres (770sq miles) of wild and remote habitat of

bamboo forest, mountains and rivers on the edge of the Tibetan Plateau.

In such a paradise, in an otherwise crowded country, maybe the panda has a chance to survive undisturbed, holding its place in the world which we all share.

THE MOUNTAIN GORILLAS OF RWANDA

Time is running out for the 'Gentle Giants' of Rwanda. Could the baby in the evocative and perhaps symbolic attitude that he takes up in my painting, apparently looking at his watch, have been thinking of his precarious future?

My wife and I were privileged to enjoy perhaps the ultimate wildlife experience a few years ago, when we spent three days in the mountainous country of the Virunga volcanoes, sitting with a family of fourteen mountain gorillas. We felt we were the intruders into their private domain, sharing with them the enjoyment, the peace and the tranquillity of undisturbed family life. A baby, a few months old, came to within touching distance, a twenty-five stone silverback walked across my legs and down the hill without even looking at me; no wonder I feel passionate about their survival.

Now we read of Rwanda, a beautiful little country, tearing itself apart in the most appalling genocide. The pristine forests in which the gorillas live are being invaded by cattle, certain areas have been mined by the rebels, and people are all the time encroaching for firewood. How long can the few hundred remaining mountain gorillas survive? It's their world too and only time will tell, but the future is full of foreboding.

INDEX